FORM 125 M

DATE			

The Chicago Public Library

Received_____

BUSINESS/SCIENCE/TECHNOLOGY
DIVISION

© THE BAKER & TAYLOR CO

The Kinked Demand Curve Analysis of Oligopoly

TO MY MOTHER AND
THE MEMORY OF
MY FATHER

The Kinked Demand Curve Analysis of Oligopoly

THEORY AND EVIDENCE

Gavin C. Reid

Edinburgh University Press

Edinburgh University Press
22 George Square, Edinburgh

ISBN 0 85224 390 1

Printed in Great Britain by
Redwood Burn Limited
Trowbridge & Esher

Contents

Contents

Chapter five

Developments of the Empirical Evidence

Chapter six

Conclusion

Preface

This study was started, as I suppose many are, by a passing curiosity in the unusual appearance of a bit of intellectual apparatus. That apparatus was, and is, what economists call the kinked demand curve theory of oligopoly. Once this passing curiosity (excited more by the oddity of the construction than anything else) had been satisfied, a deeper interest emerged. This led me to gather material that eventually became rather extensive. In this way, my own inquisitiveness became satisfied. Then a surprising thing happened. In mentioning my investigations to fellow economists, I discovered that the curiosity I had experienced was not as highly personalised a thing as I had imagined. They too were interested in where my nose had led me, and eventually I found myself acting as the supplier of too many copies of the rough drafts I had prepared on the topic. This monograph is the final product, some time later, of those drafts.

In deciding on the format of presentation to be adopted, I have been very much influenced by the surveys of theoretical and applied issues in economics that have been published in the past by the Royal Economic Society and the American Economic Association. That is, I have attempted to make the discussion comprehensible to the well-informed, non-specialist economist. It is to be hoped that this will imply that much of the material will also be accessible to those working in cognate areas, such as business studies, management science, and finance. I hope that largely I have succeeded in attaining this goal, but I am aware that at certain points the discussion becomes rather specialised, as in parts of chapter 4, whilst in other places, such as in the body of chapter 2, it is at a lower level than would suit the expert. All economists are students of the subject, but within the set of students lies a sub-set of novices that might welcome the occasional expositional digression.

To some extent, the material contained in each of the various chapters can stand alone. An especial attempt has been made to make this so in the central chapters, the second and fifth, for it was these that I felt busy readers might wish to consult without having to concern themselves with the history of the development of the theory, or with the many extensions, sometimes fairly minor, that have been accomplished. It would be impossible in a work of this kind not to incur intellectual debts to present and past generations of microeconomic theorists. A serious attempt has been made to give appropriate credit to the individuals who have developed the literature, and I have not consciously sought that form of originality that arises from ignorance of the literature. The bibliography is an integral part of this monograph, and attempts to be exhaustive, barring elementary textbook treatments. However, I am only too painfully aware that in this day and age, when every year thousands of articles are published in scores of languages in hundreds of journals, some items may have been overlooked. It is my earnest hope, however, that the coverage approaches to being comprehensive, and that at those points where no specific acknowledgments are mentioned the author has himself made at least some contribution to the breaking of new ground in a critical or constructive sense.

Of the many writers mentioned in this monograph, one in particular is pre-eminent – George Stigler. It should be unsurprising to those familiar with his works, that in his two contributions to the literature with which this monograph is concerned he has managed to write the last of the first words, and what threatens to be the first of the last words, on the topic of the kinked demand curve. Although parts of this monograph are occasionally not uncritical of his work, it is hoped that they are not unkind. It is the lot of the eminent to be plagued by 'the critic and whippersnapper', and undoubtedly when the history of economic analysis in the twentieth century is told the enormous contribution of George Stigler to microeconomic analysis will be recognised.

Other intellectual debts I owe are to Charles Hitch and Paul

Sweezy, two of the originators of the kinked demand curve analysis. They were kind enough to take time out from their very busy existences to write to me about the inception of the theory. I should also express my gratitude to Professor Simon Coke, University of Edinburgh, for encouraging me to bring this project to completion. Members of the Inter-Library Loan Department of the University of Edinburgh Library have been very helpful and patient with my detective work on the more obscure items. Mention should also be made of the cordial relationship with the Edinburgh University Press that has made this publication possible. I am sure that the excellent but anonymous refereeing comments that were channelled through to me by Mr A.R. Turnbull, Secretary to the Press, have improved materially the final presentation of the book. Chris Barton has been my faithful typist and secretary for a number of years and she brought her usual efficiency and helpfulness to the preparation of various drafts. But, ultimately, my greatest debt has been to my immediate family: to my wife for her unfailing support, and to my parents for advising me so well at critical stages in my life.

G.C.R., *Edinburgh*

1

Forerunners

1.1.   *Introduction*

Of the various alternative theories of oligopoly, the kinked demand curve theory has proved to be one of the most popular. It is
frequently mentioned in discussions of oligopoly that go beyond
the elementary level, and its widespread acceptance has occurred
despite the most damaging criticisms of it by Professor George
Stigler. The theory may be explained by a few simple geometrical
devices, and amongst other things provides an explanation of the
apparent rigidity of some industrial prices. The geometry begs
for attention, involving as it does intriguing kinks and discontinuities. To many students, an understanding of this theory must
be one of the first short steps taken beyond the self-evident
geometrical devices that economists use to explain much of
elementary economic theory. Perhaps for such reasons, rather
than for its intrinsic usefulness, this theory seems to take a grip
on the minds of even the most casual students of economics.

Not only the consumers but also the producers of elementary
economic wisdom seem to have been gripped by what Stigler
(1978, 200) has called 'a piece of scripture', which is 'to be taught
. . . to be quoted in suitable contexts, but . . . not to be tampered
with'. In examining samples of textbooks on principles and price
theory, Stigler discovered that although the number of textbooks
had greatly increased, this had by no means diminished the
proportion devoting a few perfunctory pages to the theory. In the
late 1940s, close to the historical period to which the theory had
been applied, about a quarter of the books mentioned it. This
proportion increased steadily over the years, until, in the mid-
1970s, the theory was explained by about two-thirds of the text-

books. In textbook revisions the theory, once introduced, was never deleted in subsequent editions. It is now forty years since the theory was developed, and the phenomenon it was meant to explain, even granting for the moment that it was real and not a statistical artefact, belongs to quite a distant period of economic history. Yet the scripture continues to be repeated. Is the textbook reader to gather that the theory, if not applicable today, was at least good for its own time? Or should he conclude that times have not changed in factual essentials, and that the theory is as relevant now as it was when first developed?

The purpose of this monograph is to dissect the extraordinarily robust bit of apparatus called the kinked demand curve: to enquire where it came from and whether it has now been subsumed under a broader theory; to determine whether it has been (or even can be) empirically tested; and to ask whether the questions it was devised to answer in its own time are still the questions we would ask of it today. At the end of this investigation we may be in a position to ask whether it is still useful to continue the ritual of the kinked demand curve.

1.2.   *The Earliest Contributions*

Although Sweezy (1939) and Hall and Hitch (1939)[1] are usually given credit for having first developed the kinked demand curve, it has been established by Spengler (1965) that the earliest use of it was by H. G. Hayes (1928) in *Our Economic System*. In this work, Hayes (1928, 321) introduces both reflex and obtuse kinks, the former being pointed towards the origin, and the latter away from the origin. Hayes (1928, 321–7) notes that the effect of price being set at a customary level may be to make the demand curve significantly more elastic above this price than below it:

> . . . the habit of paying a certain price for a particular good tends to make the demand for it elastic above the usual price, since customers may regard an increase in a long-established price as being so unreasonable that they will refuse to purchase the good at a higher price. This is especially true if substitutes

1. Throughout this monograph the page references for Sweezy (1939) and Hall and Hitch (1939) refer to the well-known reprints in Boulding and Stigler (1953) and Wilson and Andrews (1951) respectively.

are available at the former price. But aside from the possibility of substituting another commodity, an increase in the customary price will normally reveal a marked degree of elasticity. It is because of this fact that retail dealers will often discontinue a brand of goods rather than buy it for resale at an increase above the price that has prevailed for a considerable time.

Finally Hayes (1928, 328) introduces the complete kinked demand curve with the diagram reproduced below as figure 1.1.

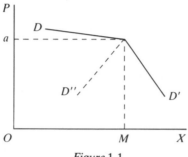

Figure 1.1

The customary price is *Oa*, and the demand curve *DD'* is highly elastic above it, and, Hayes argues, very inelastic below it. It is argued that such a demand curve exists for anthracite coal, which is interesting in view of the early use by Sweezy (1938) of a kinked demand curve for coal. Hayes argues that if price were raised appreciably then substitutes for anthracite, including, especially, bituminous coal, would be purchased. For price cuts below the customary level there would be no appreciable increase in the sale. Thus Hayes implicitly establishes a basis for price rigidity, for 'sellers tend to lose if they attempt to raise price, or if they lower the price'. Actually, though Hayes provides a correct theoretical rationale for price rigidity, Spengler cites evidence suggesting that for the case in question price rigidity was more probably caused by the anthracite coal combination. Two other features of Hayes's analysis are noteworthy. The first is that he realises that the demand curve for a single firm may be kinked, even though that for the industry is not. The second is that he is aware that the demand curve may even have a positive elasticity below the established price: a possibility later

3

recognised by Bronfenbrenner (1940). This is illustrated by the line D'' in figure 1.1. According to Hayes, such a curve might be the consequence of a tendency to judge quality by price. Spengler (1965) sets down preconditions necessary for the kinked demand curve to emerge, but his argument is highly speculative. The most plausible of Spengler's speculations is that the use by Hayes (1928, 308–14) of discontinuous demand and supply curves caused by bargaining ranges may have made him receptive to the notion of a kinked demand curve. This analysis was borrowed by Hayes from F.M.Taylor, but can be traced further back to Menger and Böhm-Bawerk. Quite possibly an economist with this Austrian influence would have found the notion of discontinuity more acceptable than one enslaved to the Marshallian dictum of *natura non facit saltum*.

Other forerunners of Hall, Hitch and Sweezy include Viner (1921), Zeuthen (1930), Robinson (1933) and Smith (1935). Of these, only Mrs Robinson's treatment is really relevant. It embraces what will be described as *obtuse* and *reflex* kinks in chapter 2. She explains the more familiar obtuse kink (pointed away from the origin, as is DD' in figure 1.1) by the tendency of a monopolist to induce entry if price is raised too much and thus, beyond a certain price, to render the demand curve highly elastic. Her treatment also gives the appropriate marginal revenue curves to the kinked curves. The marginal revenue curve was a new device at this time, and though it provides but one way of characterising an optimum, when considered jointly with marginal cost, it has proved to be one of the most useful.

Until Spengler pointed out the contribution of Hayes, it had generally been assumed that there had been no precursors of the kinked demand curve theory. This section has clearly shown that this view was mistaken. However, it appears that the treatment of Hayes was uninfluential. His treatment of demand in general is rather unsatisfactory and contains a number of confusions and errors of which the most conspicuous is a tendency to identify slope with elasticity. In truth the analytical skill required to formulate a kinked demand curve in the 1930s was not of a very high order given the right focus of attention. That is, the idea might well have emerged from the mind of many an economist, with or without the aid of Hayes. What provided the impetus for

4

the development of such a tool? Most clearly, in the case of Sweezy, and partly also in the case of Hall and Hitch, the tool appeared to throw light on the debate concerning price flexibility. One of the major issues of the day was whether or not a policy directed towards promoting price flexibility would ameliorate the unemployment of physical and human resources. In the next section a conspectus of this issue will be given, although it would wander too far from our chosen course to analyse it in any depth.

1.3.   *The Price Flexibility Debate*

Sweezy (1937) took his first step towards the kinked demand theory almost incidentally, in his concern to examine the consequences of price rigidity for the labour market. This concern with the inflexibility of some prices was pervasive amongst economists in the late 1930s, and it is a remarkable fact that one man, Gardiner Means, was largely responsible for this. Although Mills (1927) should be accredited with having undertaken the first large scale investigation into the flexibility of industrial prices in the United States, it was Means (1935, 1936) who created a major policy debate out of his own investigations on the same topic. In the monograph *Industrial Prices and their Relative Inflexibility* Means (1935, 1) introduced his celebrated doctrine of *administered prices* with the words:

> We have an administered price when a company maintains a posted price at which it will make sales or simply has its own prices at which buyers may purchase or not as they wish. Thus, when the General Motors management sets its wholesale prices for a particular model and holds that price for 6 months or a year the price is an administered price. Many wholesale and most retail prices are administered rather than market prices. For administered prices the price is rigid, at least for a period of time, and sales (and usually production) fluctuate with demand at the rigid price.

Mills (1927, 381) had tabulated frequency distributions of changes in monthly wholesale prices for seven-year periods from 1890 to 1921, for 1922–25 and for 1890–1925 (excluding 1914–1921). He found a u-shaped distribution in each case, meaning that typically prices change rather infrequently or rather often, with a moderate number of price changes being less common. It

was remarked that such distributions were curious, but no implications of a policy type were drawn, and this aspect of the study
was uninfluential. Means (1935) undertook a very similar exercise. He tabulated the frequency of price changes for 747 items
making up the BLS's wholesale price index (with only a few
omissions) for the period 1926 to 1933 with the result shown in
figure 1.2, which is adapted from the original study. Like Mills,
Means had discovered a U-shaped distribution, but what made
the two studies remarkably different in impact was the interpretation that Means put on his results. Means identified the prices
that changed infrequently with administered prices, and then
proceeded to argue that it was the existence and increasing
importance of such prices that was destroying the effective func-
tioning of the American economy.

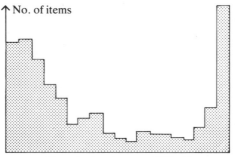

No. of price changes, 1926–33

Figure 1.2

An inspection of the tables drawn by Means's precursor, Fred-
erick Mills, shows rather similar U-shaped distributions of price
changes for seven-year sub-periods going back to 1890. Humphrey (1937) gave a detailed breakdown of price changes, which
indicated a broadly similar pattern of price rigidity from 1890–
1933, excepting the years of the First World War. If families of
price changes are distinguished, then different distributions
emerge, each of which is fairly stable period by period. For
example, the distribution of changes for finished goods had a
reversed J-shape for seven-year sub-intervals back to 1890, whilst
that for raw materials had a J-shape. On purely analytical, rather
than empirical, grounds, Scitovsky (1941) has argued that the

U-shaped distributions of Means and Mills may only be a consequence of the grouping procedure adopted. If all *within* monthly price changes were accounted for in the distribution, the modal group to the right of the U would vanish, and the distribution would assume a flattened reversed-J shape. In short, the U-shaped distribution found for month-to-month price changes may not faithfully reflect the underlying distribution of actual price changes.

Tucker (1938) introduced additional empirical content into the debate by utilising data compiled by Bezanson *et al.* (1936) on Philadelphia wholesale prices. The data were shown to indicate the existence of relatively rigid prices for finished goods right back to the eighteenth century, at which time many of these goods were produced by small-scale industries, rather than by the large-scale industries that Means felt had encouraged the development of administered prices. Furthermore, for the particular data that he was using, which were gathered during a period when the development of organised markets was rapid, Tucker was even able to detect signs of a trend to increased price flexibility. Mason (1938) reiterated and amplified some of the arguments advanced by Humphrey and Tucker, but was more sceptical of the possibility of ever reaching any conclusion about the trend in price rigidity, both because of the lack of data and also because of the quality changes that so many goods undergo over time. He was also critical of the examination of price flexibility purely mechanically in terms of the frequency of price changes. Flexibility only makes sense as a concept when used in relation to some yardstick. Mason argued that the important point to consider was the extent to which price varied in response to various determining factors. Even then a number of measures, including, for example, the price flexibility coefficient of Moore (1922), which is the reciprocal of the elasticity of demand, might be appropriate, depending on the purpose at hand. This is a theme that will be revisited in chapter 5, which is concerned with the consequences for price flexibility of the kinked demand curve. Mason's concept of price flexibility, as a relationship between price and changes in other economic variables, will prove to be germane to that discussion.

Although the arguments presented by Means (1935, 1936) be-

7

came widely accepted, particularly in policy circles and in public debate, it has been shown in this section that even in its own time the scientific basis for his arguments did not go unchallenged. The debate has been reopened on several occasions since then, especially by George Stigler, and most notably in the important study on transaction (as opposed to list) prices by Stigler and Kindahl (1970). The issue will never be closed, but undoubtedly the distinction between rigid and flexible prices is much less clear than Means suggested, and, further, the supposed historical trend to the predominance of markets with administered prices is questionable. Thus the kinked demand curve as an analytical tool may have been developed to explain a statistical tendency that was not as well established as might have been apparent at first sight.

1.4. *Early Views on the Causes of Price Rigidity*

The last section has argued that the thesis that Means advanced concerning the historical trend of price rigidity was misleading, if not entirely wrong. What has not been denied is that some prices are relatively more rigid than others, and that these prices tend to be for manufactured goods. Thus in the 1930s there remained a need, as perhaps there had been in previous periods, for a satisfactory explanation of price rigidity. In earlier pages, it has been suggested that one of the reasons why the kinked demand curve emerged was to provide a possible explanation for price rigidity. However, it need not be the *only* explanation; a point to be borne in mind when undertaking empirical tests of the kinked demand curve. In this section, some early views on the causes of price rigidity will be examined, because some of them anticipate or complement the kinked demand curve theory, and also because some provide quite different, and in the proper context, equally valid explanations of price rigidity. Of course the existence, in itself, of any alternative explanation in no way invalidates the kinked demand curve.

Means (1935, 20) argued that the system developed by the classical economists was no longer useful, saying that 'this theory was set forth by Adam Smith to explain the workings of an economy quite different from that now existing'. In fact, as Tucker (1938) has pointed out, Smith, Ricardo and Mill were all

8

aware of the existence of price rigidities (for indeed this was an historical fact), and, furthermore, had views on its causes. For example, Adam Smith (1776, 60–1, 117–18) was aware of the different price behaviour to be expected in agricultural, as compared to manufacturing, activity. In Smith's view price tended to fluctuate considerably about the 'natural price' in the former case, and to lie close to it in the latter. In the short run (or market) period, prices varied to clear markets, but in the long run price was determined by rent, wages and raw materials costs, and markets were cleared by quantity variation. Mill (1848, 310–12) was aware of the influence that habit, accident and ignorance could have in maintaining a price rigidly at some customary level. Marshall (1920, 377), strictly a neoclassical rather than a classical writer, talked of the fear of 'spoiling the market', which would exercise a controlling influence over short-run price variation. Thus it is apparent that by the 1930s sufficient attention had already been given to price rigidity to support the view that a body of received knowledge on the topic existed. To an extent, therefore, views on price rigidity generated by the debate of the 1930s constituted an addition to, and amendment of, established economic wisdom.

Logically, our discussion should start with the man who generated the price flexibility debate. As well as providing statistical evidence of price rigidity, Means also attempted to explain it. He did so by appealing to two factors: the development of the technology of manufacturing; and the growth in industrial concentration. The way these factors interact to produce rigidity is best illustrated by the example given by Means (1935, 24–5) of the pricing of Chevrolets compared to the pricing of carrots. The farmer does not know what price his carrots will fetch, but is certain that he would rather sell them than have to ship them back from market to rot on his own hands. The producers of Chevrolets decide ahead on the list price for a certain year and circulate it to salesmen. They have in mind an expected (but uncertain) level of production, and a certain price. This price is set at a level that, based on contractual commitments to certain input costs, will provide an acceptable profit on each car sold. If demand falls in the agricultural type of market, price also falls. But in the industrial type of market, it is argued, price is held

9

constant in the face of a fall in demand, with the consequence that production falls. The burden of overheads increases the unit cost of production, but firms are reluctant to raise price (to cover costs) in what is perceived as a falling market, and even less inclined to reduce price in the face of falling revenue. Means (1935, 11, 33) argues that 'The amount by which he can count on increasing his sales by lowering price is usually so small that the whole balance of his interest as a business man points towards a restriction of output', and in similar vein, 'the net income on the increment of sales due to lower price all too often would not make up for the loss in income due to the lower price on the sale already in prospect'. These words foreshadow the argument later advanced for the lower branch of the kinked demand curve, but Means apparently dismisses as irrational the possibility that price might be raised. His argument is superficially like the idea that goods with administered prices are in inelastic demand for price reductions, but is in reality more complex, for it refers not to movements along any given demand function, but to a succession of points on a series of leftward-shifting demand curves. Humphrey (1937) argued that the relative rigidity of industrial, as compared to agricultural prices, was no new phenomenon, and did not need to be connected with the growth of large-scale enterprise. To him it is a consequence of two factors: first, that the output of farmers is very closely controlled because of the natural crop period; and secondly, that wage labour is a more important component of manufacturing than of agricultural cost, and wage labour is not as easily changed as is the farmer's (implicit) wage.

However, it had earlier been pointed out by Galbraith (1936) that some industrial costs, such as those for certain raw materials and agricultural products, might be more flexible than some agricultural costs, a fact that weakens the force of Humphrey's second argument. Thus the view that rigid costs cause rigid product prices is not entirely convincing, and the role of concentration remains to be investigated. Means did not argue that monopoly *per se* caused price rigidity, nor did he deny that administered prices might exist in markets that could be described as competitive in the broad sense of the word. His view was that increased concentration, undertaken in order to reap the benefits of the division of labour, had led to improvements in technology. Modern production methods, which required the co-ordination of many functions, such as the meshing of sales and raw materials contracts, encouraged the use of administered prices. Means was aware that under the traditional conception of monopoly, as described, for example, by Cournot, shifts in demand and/or cost would be reflected in price variation. Further, he remarked that in industries that were not monopolised, but subject to rigorous competition amongst few producers, prices might be administered, and hence prone to rigidity. It was for just such market situations that the kinked demand curve theory was to be devised.

Means's 'theory' of price rigidity is rather diffuse by contrast to the kinked demand curve theory. He argued that technological change goes hand-in-hand with the division of labour, and that a desire to exploit more fully the benefits of the division of labour would result in increasing industrial concentration. In this process there is a shift from market to administered pricing. The weakness of Means's argument is that one is never really sure what constitutes administered pricing. It seems that the term is really a catch-all phrase, which covers a number of possible sources of price rigidity. Something akin to an elasticities argument for price rigidity has already been discussed, but in the writings of Means (1935, 1936) other arguments for price rigidity also parade under the umbrella of administered pricing. At one point, Means suggests that price rigidity is the outcome of the problems of administrative co-ordination in a large firm, as though a rigid price were a useful rule of thumb in a complex world. At another, price is said to be held at a certain level by tacit agreement amongst those in the market who operate under similar conditions. At yet another, the cost of making price changes in modern market conditions is preferred as a cause of price rigidity. Certainly these are all possible factors promoting price rigidity, but they do not really constitute a coherent theory of price rigidity.

A serious attempt to provide a comprehensive analysis of causes of price rigidity was undertaken by Galbraith (1936), but not with unqualified success. He became an enthusiastic supporter of Means's doctrine, but pushed it further in arguing that monopoly

11

in a broadly defined sense was indeed a cause of price rigidity. This position appears to be at variance with Means, who argued that monopoly did not cause price rigidity; but in reality the clash is slight, for Galbraith worked with a far-ranging concept of monopoly. In Galbraith's terminology 'monopoly power' is vested in any producer who can control supply and price, whether he be a pure monopolist, duopolist, oligopolist or monopolistic competitor. A number of his 'proofs' that price rigidity must be caused by monopoly power are distinctly tautological in flavour. For example, Galbraith (1936, 460) argued that pure competition is the only market form not subject to monopoly power. Under pure competition, reduced demand would entail a reduced output *and* price. *Ergo* price rigidity can only occur in the presence of monopoly power. He repeated a number of familiar arguments for price rigidity, including custom (Mill) and fear of spoiling the market (Marshall). A notable feature of his work was the emphasis on the transition process. Galbraith looked at the adjustment process consequential on a decrease in demand, in industries subject to pure competition as compared to monopoly power. His argument is that under pure competition the initial impact of a decrease in demand would be a fall in price that would exceed that which would prevail in the longer run, when full adjustment, involving presumably the exit of firms, had been made. If monopoly power is present, and firms are interdependent, the argument is that group interest will ensure that the adjustment of price will be more gentle, and will not overshoot and then return to its new equilibrium position. At another point, Galbraith argued that in impure competition the process of price adjustment might be impeded by frictions that are at root caused by imperfections of information. This emphasis on rigidities inherent in the adjustment process, rather than on equilibrium positions, is perceptive, though almost incidental to the main thrust of his argument. Galbraith devoted much more attention to attempting to prove that price would move more for a demand reduction under pure competition than under monopoly power. He gave a tortuous discussion of that issue, which Scitovsky (1941) later proved to be faulty. In fact, no conclusion can be drawn for the general case, but for a special case Scitovsky (1941) was able to demonstrate that price would be more flexible under monopoly than under pure competition. Some time later, Niehans (1958) provided a detailed taxonomy of the various consequences for price rigidity entailed by adopting differing assumptions about the concavity and convexity of demand and cost curves, but nevertheless confirmed the conclusion that nothing could be said of the general case.

Finally, apart from the above arguments, Galbraith mentioned a number of 'incentives to price rigidity'. These were four business habits: first, the tendency to tacit or formal agreement to protect the group interest; secondly, the tendency to favour retail price maintenance in markets for differentiated products; thirdly, the tendency to base price on average cost, especially when prime costs are rigid; and fourthly, the tendency for a monopolist to become 'fat' and subject to inertia. One, or several, of these had been mentioned by previous writers, including Means, and they do not constitute an analytical theory of price rigidity, coming as they do under the heading of 'habits'.

To conclude, it is apparent that during the greater part of the 1930s no satisfactory theoretical exploration of price rigidity had been developed. In some cases, the arguments of classical economists were revived or rediscovered; in others, the components of a theory were set out but not developed. The inevitable impression created is of a profession in a state of confusion over the price flexibility debate, but one that was vainly searching for a satisfactory analytical explanation for price rigidity. By 1939, that theory was to be presented to the profession by Hall, Hitch and Sweezy in the form of the kinked demand curve analysis of oligopoly. As the opening words of this chapter indicated, it is a theory that has remained with the profession ever since.

The Elementary Analytics of
the Kinked Demand Curve

2.1.   *Introduction*

The purpose of this chapter is to explain in elementary terms, using no more than simple algebra and diagrams, the analytical properties of kinked demand curves. Students of economics, and even some professional economists, seem to be very much at sea when the possibility of a discontinuity in any of the familiar curves arises. In reality, as the early marginalists like Menger and Wicksteed emphasised, marginalism can cope quite adequately with the finite jumps possessed by some of the curves used by economists.

Without yet investigating problems of interpreting and extending the kinked demand curve model, it will prove useful to work through the bare bones of the analytics of kinked curves. In later chapters, more complex problems will be tackled, but they will by and large prove to be direct extensions of the ideas now to be developed.

The treatment is unashamedly elementary and flat-footed, though the number of times the author has repeated it on the blackboard in his room for students and staff alike makes him hopeful that it may prove useful to the less experienced reader. More experienced or expert readers may skim the diagrams of this chapter and then jump to the appendix, which deals with the matters treated in the main body of the text with reasonable terseness.

2.2.   *Kinks, Gaps and Discontinuities*

In many areas of microeconomic theory, the demand curves are smooth and free from gaps. In the present treatment, a demand

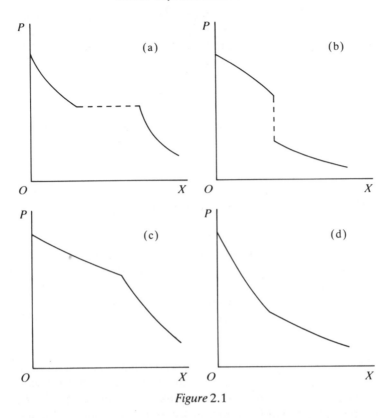

Figure 2.1

curve may have a *gap*, in which case for a particular demand price there is a range over which quantity demanded is not defined; it may have a *discontinuity*, in which case demand price is not defined over a certain range for a particular quantity demanded; and it may have a *kink*, in which case it is either of the *obtuse kink* or *reflex kink* variety. Demand curves with gaps or discontinuities arise naturally in several areas of analytical microeconomics, for example in the characteristics approach to demand theory of Lancaster (1966), in the contingent demand curve theory of Shubik (1959) and in the work of the author himself, Reid (1975, 1977). As will become evident in later chapters, such demand curves bear a strong family resemblance to the various forms of kinked demand curves.

In figure 2.1, diagram (a) illustrates a *gap*, (b) illustrates a *discontinuity*, (c) illustrates an *obtuse kink*, and (d) illustrates a *reflex kink*. The convenient terms of 'obtuse kink' and 'reflex kink' are due to Efroymson (1943), and these concepts will also be referred to in this book as the *normal kink* and the *reverse* (or *reversed*) *kink*. In more complex analytical settings, such as those discussed by Reid (1975) and Shapley and Shubik (1969), demand curves may possess various combinations of the characteristics exhibited in figure 2.1, but for the moment only (c) and (d), the obtuse kink and the reflex kink, will be investigated. For simplicity, it will generally be assumed that over those ranges for which a demand curve is defined, to each price there is but one quantity, and to each quantity there is but one price.

2.3.   *Kinked Demand Curves*

The important characteristic of a kink in a demand curve is that at such a point there is a jump in the rate at which revenue is changing with respect to quantity. Expressed alternatively, there is a discontinuity in the marginal revenue curve. That this is so is sometimes a puzzle to students of economics, but the situation is readily clarified by reference to figure 2.2. In this diagram there are two linear demand curves, DE and AB, which can be used to make up the two basic types of kinked demand curves. For the obtuse kink the segments DI and IB constitute the relevant demand curve; and for the reflex kink, the segments AI and IE are relevant. It will be found useful to look on kinked demand curves as being made up of such segments, for at a later stage it will be shown how the kinked demand curve can be regarded as consisting of different segments of the famous dd' and DD' demand curves of Edward Chamberlin (1933). A well-known result of microeconomic theory, explained for example by Allen (1962, ch. 14), is that a linear demand curve has a linear marginal revenue curve that is equidistant from the price axis and the demand curve. Thus in figure 2.2, $OC = CB$ and $OF = FE$, where AC and DF are the marginal revenue curves corresponding to the demand curves AB and DE respectively. For the obtuse kink (DIB) the two relevant marginal revenue segments are DH (for quantities demanded up to amount x_0) and GC (for quantities demanded greater than x_0). Strictly speaking, marginal revenue

16

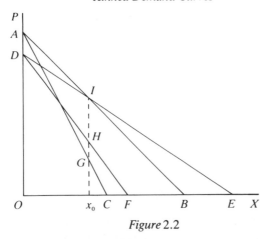

Figure 2.2

becomes negative beyond C. It should be noticed that this construction implies a discontinuity in the marginal revenue curve for DIB, this being of magnitude HG. For the reflex kink AIE, the marginal revenue curve is made up of segments AG and HF, with the discontinuity being HG. The same general pattern can be shown to obtain for kinked demand curves with non-linear segments, as indicated for example by Joan Robinson (1933, ch. 2). These two general shapes, which will be referred to frequently in subsequent discussion, are given in diagrams (a) and (b) of figure 2.3, where AR and MR denote average revenue and marginal revenue.

To conclude this section, a standard result on the elasticities of obtuse kinked demand curves can be made plausible by reference to figure 2.2. For the formal proof, due to Stigler (1947), the reader is referred to the appendix to this chapter. Denoting the elasticities at I for the linear demand curves DIE and AIB by η_1 and η_2 we have

$$\eta_1 = \frac{x_0 E}{O x_0} \quad \text{and} \quad \eta_2 = \frac{x_0 B}{O x_0}$$

using a standard result in microeconomic theory, as explained in Allen (1962, ch. 16) for example. But $x_0 E > x_0 B$ whence $\eta_1 > \eta_2$. Now considering the obtuse kinked demand curve DIB, with η_1 the relevant elasticity for segment DI and η_2 the relevant one for

17

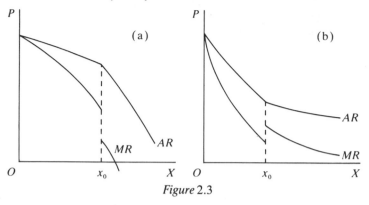

Figure 2.3

segment IB, it is clear that the closer E becomes to B, by pivoting DE about I, the smaller the discontinuity HG becomes. But the closer E is to B, the closer η_2 is to η_1. That is, the lesser is the difference between the elasticities of the two segments of the obtuse kink, the lesser is the discontinuity in the marginal revenue curve and vice versa.

2.4.   *Revenue and Cost Curves*

For the purposes of later discussion, especially on the comparative statics properties of the kinked demand curve model, it will be useful to have an appreciation of the general shape of the total revenue curves implied by the kinked demand curves. For a straight line demand curve falling downwards from left to right, the total revenue curve is a quadratic function, being concave when viewed from the origin, passing through the origin and a positive quantity on the horizontal axis, and being symmetric about the quantity at which total revenue attains a maximum. For more general downward sloping demand curves, the total revenue curve can assume a variety of shapes, although it is generally assumed (at least) that it is concave. The point on the quantity axis at which total revenue reaches a maximum must also be the point at which marginal revenue becomes zero, assuming a smooth approach to the maximum. However if the maximum of the total revenue curve is of the form of a pointed peak or cusp, then marginal revenue must be positive to the left, and negative to the right, of the point on the quantity axis at

18

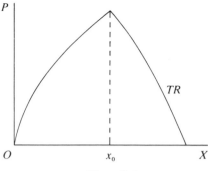

Figure 2.4

which the maximum is achieved. The most general criterion for a maximum, and certainly the most useful if kinks, plateaux and discontinuities may be involved, is that changes in the value of a function should be negative, for positive and negative variations about the point at which the maximum is achieved. To be more concrete, consider the case of a revenue function which depends on quantity per unit time, x, and denote this function $R(x)$. Then x_0 will be the point at which this function reaches a maximum if, for greater and lesser values of x_0, the function evaluated for such values is less than $R(x_0)$. In the case in which the marginal revenue curve for the obtuse kinked demand curve has a discontinuity that extends right down to the quantity axis (i.e. for which a segment such as GC in figure 2.2 is everywhere below the quantity axis) the total revenue curve (TR) has the form shown in figure 2.4. Although conventional calculus methods are inappropriate for revealing x_0 as the maximum for this revenue function, the simple criterion mentioned above will do the trick. This sort of peaked total revenue curve has been popularised by the paper of Shepherd (1962) on the sales maximisation model of Baumol (1958), and it has since been extensively used in the textbook treatment of Heidensohn and Robinson (1974). The curve is convenient, because it will generally induce a similar peak in the profit function; and one might then argue, as Shepherd has done, that a sales revenue maximiser will choose the same output as a profit maximiser. However, this form of revenue function is a rather special case, and not the one that

19

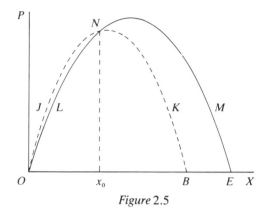

Figure 2.5

emerges most naturally from the obtuse and reflex kinked demand curves. Revenue functions for the curves in figure 2.2 are given in figure 2.5, where x_0, B and E have the same interpretation in each diagram. The total revenue curve for the demand curve AB is JNK, and LNM is the total revenue curve for the demand curve DE. Therefore the total revenue curves for the two kinked demand curves are hybrids of JNK and LNM. For the obtuse kink DIB, the corresponding total revenue curve is LNK, and for the reflex kink it is JNM, the point N being a kink in the revenue curve in each case. It should be noticed that LNK differs from the shape shown in figure 2.4, and that JNM even has a non-concave section in the locality of N.

2.5.   *Optimality Conditions*

Whether or not the optimality conditions considered in this section are defined in terms of objective or subjective conditions is dependent on the extent and quality of information available to firms. In the extreme case of very full information and unlimited information processing capabilities, there is some sense in regarding the optimality conditions as objectively defined. Given this assumption on knowledge, objectively defined kinked demand curves can be constructed using the device of *contingent demand curves*, as developed in chapter 4 below. If weaker assumptions on knowledge are adopted, then the interpretation adopted by writers such as Machlup (1946, 1952) is worthy of consideration. Proponents of this view emphasise the extreme difficulty of determining individual equilibrium for the firm, given limitations on information, and regard the more useful role of marginalism as being the consideration of how firms will react to exogenous changes. However, they do accept the usefulness of concepts such as (subjective) marginal cost and (subjective) marginal revenue, and the equivalence, in a tautological sense, of the propositions 'maximise profit' and 'equate marginal cost with marginal revenue'. Therefore, in discussing optimality conditions it is acceptable to adopt the objective or subjective approach, bearing in mind the different interpretations of the state of information lying behind each approach. However, this flexibility of interpretation cannot mask the fact that a principal limitation of discussions couched in the terms developed below is an inadequate treatment of the problems of knowledge.

The construction of the kinked demand curve model only becomes complete once costs have been introduced. For the moment, it will be assumed that in the obtuse kink case the marginal cost curve goes through the discontinuous section of the marginal revenue curve, without yet enquiring whether it *must*, or whether it merely *may* do so. In the case of the reflex kinked demand curve, it will be assumed that the marginal cost curve cuts each branch of the marginal revenue curve once, and also goes through the discontinuity. These two cases are illustrated in the upper diagrams (a) and (b) of figure 2.6. In the lower diagrams (c) and (d), the corresponding profit functions (Π) are shown. Denoting profit by Π, total revenue by R, total cost by C, and assuming these are each functions of quantity per unit time, x, the profit function may be written:

$$\Pi(x) = R(x) - C(x) \tag{2.1}$$

For a maximum, it is required that

$$\Delta\Pi = (\Delta R - \Delta C) < 0 \quad \text{for} \quad \Delta x \gtrless 0 \tag{2.2}$$

That is, changes in profit must be in the downward direction for positive and negative variations in quantity per unit time about the optimal point. Dividing both sides of (2.2) by a positive Δx gives

21

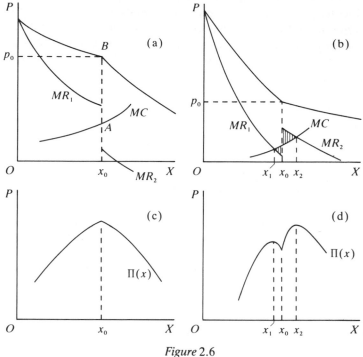

Figure 2.6

$$\left\{\frac{\Delta R}{\Delta x} - \frac{\Delta C}{\Delta x}\right\} < 0 \text{ or } \frac{\Delta R}{\Delta x} < \frac{\Delta C}{\Delta x} \text{ for } \Delta x > 0 \qquad (2.3)$$

Proceeding similarly for a negative Δx, and remembering that dividing both sides of an inequality by a negative number reverses the sign of the inequality, gives

$$\frac{\Delta R}{\Delta x} > \frac{\Delta C}{\Delta x} \text{ for } \Delta x < 0 \qquad (2.4)$$

More simply,

$$MR \gtreqless MC \text{ for } \Delta x \lesseqgtr 0 \qquad (2.5)$$

where MR and MC denote marginal revenue and marginal cost, respectively. The optimality criterion given by (2.5) applies whether or not the profit function is differentiable. It requires

22

that for negative variation about the maximum, marginal revenue exceeds marginal cost, and that for positive variation, marginal cost exceeds marginal revenue. It is clear that the curves of figure 2.6(a) satisfy the criterion for a profit maximum at x_0. Calculus methods cannot be applied to the corresponding profit function in figure 2.6(c), for this function comes to a sharp point, or more properly, is not differentiable, at x_0. Thus the normal $MR = MC$ criterion relevant to everywhere differentiable functions is inapplicable to this case, and it is quite wrong to assert, as some authors do, that the kink represents the point at which marginal revenue and marginal cost are most nearly equal. It is also quite wrong to 'draw in' the marginal revenue curve along the vertical jump, and then to assert that the $MR = MC$ criterion still applies. These are not mistakes, incidentally, that the originators of the idea perpetrated, but they are widespread in current textbook treatments. In the case of smooth functions, Lerner's *degree of monopoly* is easily shown to be equal to the reciprocal of the elasticity of demand. Unfortunately there is no unique elasticity at the price p_0, but as Lange (1944, 41) points out, the degree of monopoly may still be defined, it being given by AB/x_0B in figure 2.6(a).

Figure 2.6(b) illustrates the reflex kink that Efroymson (1943, 1955) has suggested might apply when firms are operating close to capacity. By the criterion (2.5), so-called 'local' maxima exist at x_1 and x_2. By appropriately reversing the argument that led to (2.5) it will be clear that profit achieves a (local) minimum at x_0. This minimum occurs at a kink in the profit function, as indicated in figure 2.6(d). It could not be detected by calculus methods, whereas the local maxima at x_1 and x_2 *could*, and the usual $MC = MR$ criterion applies for these points, with second-order conditions being used to check for a maximum.

Whether the maximum maximorum or 'global' maximum is located at x_1 or x_2 is easily discovered by using a device employed by Joan Robinson (1933, ch. 3). Profit at any output level is equal to the area contained between the marginal revenue and marginal cost curves, due respect being paid to sign (i.e. if marginal cost exceeds marginal revenue over a range of output, profit is negative over that range). In figure 2.6(b), the decrease in profit in moving from x_1 to x_0 (measured by the roughly triangular area between MR and MC shaded-in over this range) is exceeded by the addition to profit for the larger shaded area over the range x_0 to x_2. Thus profit achieves a global maximum at x_2.

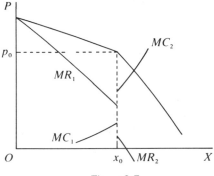

Figure 2.7

Finally, an interesting application of the optimality criterion (2.5) is to the case in which the marginal cost curve is also kinked: the case of oligopsony, which will be discussed further in chapter 4. In this case, the obtuse kinked demand curve model has the appearance indicated in figure 2.7. For negative variations about x_0, $MR_1 > MC_1$, and for positive variations $MC_2 > MR_2$. Thus the optimality criterion is satisfied, and x_0 is the profit maximising output even when both the marginal cost and marginal revenue curves are kinked.

Appendix
The Analytics of the Kinked Demand Curve

1. *Functional Relationships.* The symbols adopted are: average revenue (AR); marginal revenue (MR); total revenue (R); profit (Π); total cost (C); quantity per unit time (x); price per unit (p).

Any kinked demand curve may be regarded as an average revenue function made up of two branches, each of which is negatively sloped, and each having one point (p_0, x_0) in common:

$$AR \equiv f(x) = f_1(x), \ x \leq x_0, \ f_1' < 0$$
$$= f_2(x), \ x \geq x_0, \ f_2' < 0$$

AR is continuous, that is

$$f(x_0) = f_1(x_0) = f_2(x_0) = p_0$$

but is not smooth, there being a kink at (p_0, x_0). That is, there is a discontinuity in the demand function $d(AR)/dx$ at x_0:

$$\lim_{x \to x_0^-} f_1'(x) \neq \lim_{x \to x_0^+} f_2'(x)$$

This may be expressed more simply as:

$$f_1'(x_0) \neq f_2'(x_0)$$

In general $f_1'(x_0)$, when used on its own or in other expressions, will be understood to be defined by an appropriate left-hand or right-hand derivative. In terms of the literature, two types of kinked demand curves have been discussed:

(a) The obtuse, or normal, for which $f_1'(x_0) > f_2'(x_0)$.

(b) The reflex, or reverse, for which $f_1'(x_0) < f_2'(x_0)$.

Note that in the everyday parlance of the economist, the upper segment f_1 of the obtusely kinked demand curve is described as being more elastic than the lower segment f_2, by virtue of the fact that $f_1'(x_0) > f_2'(x_0)$ implies

$$\left| \frac{p_0}{x_0} \cdot \frac{1}{f_1'(x_0)} \right| > \left| \frac{p_0}{x_0} \cdot \frac{1}{f_2'(x_0)} \right| \text{ or } |\eta_1| > |\eta_2|$$

where η_1 and η_2 are the elasticities of demand, of the upper and lower segments. The total and marginal revenue curves are given by:

$R = xf(x)$ and $MR = dR/dx$,

from which

$$MR = MR_1(x) = x_1 f_1'(x) + f_1(x) \text{ for } x \leq x_0$$
$$= MR_2(x) = x_2 f_2'(x) + f_2(x) \text{ for } x \geq x_0$$

In general, MR_1 and MR_2 will not meet at x_0 because $f_1'(x_0) \neq f_2'(x_0)$. The length of the discontinuity is given by:

$$MR_1(x_0) - MR_2(x_0) = x_0 f_1'(x_0) + f_1(x_0) - x_0 f_2'(x_0) - f_2(x_0)$$
$$= x_0 f_1'(x_0) - x_0 f_2'(x_0)$$
$$= p_0 \left[\frac{x_0 f_1'(x_0)}{p_0} - \frac{x_0 f_2'(x_0)}{p_0} \right]$$
$$= p_0 \left[\frac{1}{\eta_1} - \frac{1}{\eta_2} \right]$$

where η_1 and η_2 are the demand elasticities of the upper and lower branches, evaluated at x_0. This formula was first given by Stigler (1947). A direct consequence is that

$$|MR_1(x_0) - MR_2(x_0)| \to 0 \text{ as } \eta_1 \to \eta_2$$

a property first observed by Sweezy (1939).

2. *Geometry*. (a) In the obtuse (normal) kink case $f_1'(x_0) > f_2'(x_0)$, whence, in view of the formula proved in section 1,

$$[MR_1(x_0) - MR_2(x_0)] > 0, \text{ that is } MR_1 > MR_2$$

This is illustrated in figure 2.6(a) in the main text.

(b) In the reflex (reverse) kink case, by a converse argument, $MR_1 < MR_2$ at x_0. This is illustrated in figure 2.6(b).

3. *Optimality Conditions*. For the profit function $\Pi(x) = R(x) - C(x)$, a general condition for a maximum that does not require differentiability of the functions concerned is that

$$\Delta\Pi = (\Delta R - \Delta C) < 0 \text{ for } \Delta x \gtrless 0$$

For positive and negative increments this requires that

$$\frac{\Delta R}{\Delta x} \leqq \frac{\Delta C}{\Delta x} \text{ for } \Delta x \gtreqless 0$$

By this criterion, $\Pi(x_0)$ is a maximum for the obtuse (normal) kink illustrated in figure 2.6(a). The condition does not fail if either *MR* or *MC* have jumps. Figure 2.7 of the main text illustrates the case of oligopoly in the goods market and oligopsony in the factor market, and application of the criterion confirms that $\Pi(x_0)$ is a maximum in this case. For the reflex (reverse) kink illustrated in figure 2.6(b), $\Pi(x_1)$ and $\Pi(x_2)$ are local maxima with $\Pi''(x_1), \Pi''(x_2) < 0$, and $\Pi(x_0)$ is a local minimum, points which have been made by Stigler (1947) and Efroymson (1943). The greater of the local maxima may be discovered by a criterion mentioned by Robinson (1933) and Efroymson (1943):

$$\Pi(x_1) \gtreqless \Pi(x_2) \text{ as}$$

$$\int_{x_0}^{x_2} [MR_2(x) - MC(x)]dx \lesseqgtr \int_{x_1}^{x_0} [MC(x) - MR_1(x)]dx$$

In the case illustrated, $\Pi(x_2) > \Pi(x_1)$.

The Genesis of the Theory of
the Kinked Demand Curve

3.1.   *Introduction*

As indicated in chapter 1, the geometry of the kink was understood before 1939, and precursors of the analytics of the kink can
also be identified. However, the theory of oligopoly that is
associated with the kinked demand curve is inextricably linked
with the names of Sweezy (1939) and of Hall and Hitch (1939). It
is with the genesis of the theory that this chapter is concerned.

Though often quoted together, the theories of Sweezy and of
Hall and Hitch are distinct. Sweezy's theory is based on the
notion of imagined demand curves, and is not concerned with
providing an explanation of the level of prices. The empirical
foundations of his theory are not well secured in his article,
though doubtless various bits of corroborating evidence could
have been produced. The theory of Hall and Hitch is based on
interviews with business men, and, as well as providing an explanation of price rigidity, purports to provide an explanation of the
level at which price is set. Price, it is claimed, is a mark-up on unit
variable cost.

On the whole, the analysis of Sweezy has found greater favour
in the literature, and it is to his contribution that this chapter
turns first.

3.2.   *The Contribution of Sweezy*

Some idea of the process by which Sweezy proceeded to his 1939
article can be obtained by examining anticipations of the analysis
in Sweezy (1937, 1938). In a round table discussion on wages
policy, Sweezy (1937) argues that the best framework for ana-
lysing the effect of a general change in money wages is one based

on a theory of oligopoly rather than of perfect competition. It is argued that demand curves exist in the heads of entrepreneurs and are based on a consideration of the probable reactions of rivals. The origins of this theory will be examined shortly, but suffice it to say for the moment that Sweezy argues that the imagined demand curve would have what he calls a 'corner' at the prevailing price if entrepreneurs believed that a price cut would be self-defeating and a price rise would rapidly drive away business. He assumes the reader knows that such a demand curve would have a discontinuous marginal revenue curve (of the type described in 2.2 above) and is led to conclude that a wage cut would not lead to an increase in the volume of employment. In the scenario described by Sweezy, it is shifts in demand rather than in costs that primarily affect the volume of employment. Changes in money wages would not affect unemployment through consequential cost shifts, because of the kink, and would also have little effect on the volume of expenditure. At the time, Sweezy (1937, 157) seems to have had considerable confidence in his analysis, saying that he believed 'the real world is very much more like the model which I have analysed than the usual models'. His line of argument was refined and extended with considerable success by Oskar Lange (1944) in *Price Flexibility and Employment* – a development to which we shall return in chapter 4. In his David A. Wells prize essay, which was based on a Harvard doctoral thesis of 1937, Sweezy (1938) also uses a kinked *industry* (rather than particular) demand curve to explain the behaviour of an association of coal producers in northern England in the nineteenth century. The insights that Sweezy had gained in his informal contacts with the business community would have provided him with some concrete basis for formulating his theory of oligopoly.

Given familiarity with the conduct of certain oligopolists, and knowledge of the mathematical relationships between a kinked demand curve and its corresponding marginal revenue curve, the final component to make Sweezy's analysis complete is the Kaldorian notion of an 'imagined demand curve'. In his review of Joan Robinson's *The Economics of Imperfect Competition* (1933), Kaldor (1934) expresses doubts about the validity of the demand curve construction that Mrs Robinson used. It is Kaldor's view that the real demand curve might well be indeterminate, since it depends on the conjectures that firms make about each other's behaviour. On the other hand, an imagined demand curve, although based on incomplete information, is necessarily determinate if it can be formulated in the head of the entrepreneur.

In the degenerate case, in which the entrepreneur has no idea at all about his real demand curve, his imagined demand curve will be horizontal up to the amount sold, and then vertical. More probably, his imagined demand curve will have a series of 'steps', rather than just one 'step' as in the degenerate case, and might also have gaps, kinks and discontinuities. The estimate that an entrepreneur makes of his demand curve determines whether the price will be maintained. Of necessity the imagined and real demand curves must coincide at an equilibirium point, though this does not preclude that they coincide at other points.

The basic components of the Sweezy analysis having been assembled, the theory itself may now be examined. Sweezy presents a kinked demand curve that is sufficiently acutely kinked that the discontinuity in the marginal revenue function extends to below the quantity axis, an important case that was later to be used by Shepherd (1962) in a critique of Baumol's (1958) sales revenue maximisation hypothesis. Sweezy refers to evidence on the shape of the imagined demand curve, which may be gathered by interviewing business men, but gives no direct citation of this evidence. He argues that in depressed conditions business men will experience pleasure at a gain in business and will view with alarm a loss in business. Thus producers will not raise price for fear of loss of business and will not cut price for fear of little gain in business. As demand expands, depressed conditions are left behind and firms work closer to full capacity. This will reduce the elasticity of the upper segment of the kinked demand curve, and increase that of the lower segment as firms become less worried about the prospect of a loss in business, and more unconcerned about the consequences of a retaliatory price cut. The result of this, as the analytics of section 2.3 have shown, is a diminution of the discontinuity in the marginal revenue curve.

In a familiar way, Sweezy argues that marginal cost variations within the discontinuity in the marginal revenue curve will leave price and output unaltered in the short run. More interestingly, he suggests that this provides a defence for the argument of some trade unionists that higher wages will not affect output and price, but will merely lower profits. His discussion of varying elasticities of the upper and lower segments of the kinked demand curve is more thorough than the rather tangential remarks on this same theme by Hall and Hitch (1939) and anticipates the logical extensions of his work undertaken by Efroymson (1943, 1955). Assuming that the pressure on marginal costs is generally upwards as business conditions improve from an initial position below full capacity, the general tendency will be for prices to rise. If, instead, business conditions deteriorate further from this same initial position, the upward pressure on marginal costs will be diminished, the discontinuity in the marginal revenue curve will be increased, and there will be an even more marked tendency to price rigidity. In summary, if imagined demand curves are kinked there will be a general tendency to price rigidity, which will be ameliorated in good times to a tendency to upward price flexibility, and exacerbated in bad times to a very marked tendency to price rigidity in both upward and downward directions.

Sweezy recognises that in depressed business conditions, there would be a tendency for secret undercutting to take place. This would have the effect of increasing the elasticity of the lower segment of the kinked demand curve. In general, off-list price cutting, which attempted to exercise price discrimination among customers, would have a similar effect. Price leadership would diminish the elasticity of the kinked demand curve above the prevailing price. In his second diagram, Sweezy (1939, 407) illustrates the two separate cases on the same figure, presenting a reflexively kinked curve that is sometimes confused with a related device introduced by Efroymson (1943). In fact, Sweezy's diagram merely economises on graphics and does not have the Efroymson interpretation. In the presence of price leadership, followers are presumed to be just as willing to follow price increases (the case illustrated by Sweezy) as price decreases, and this would tend to smooth out the kink. In the case of secret price cutting (also represented on the same diagram by Sweezy) there is a relatively elastic demand response to pricing below the established, or list, level.

Sweezy (1939, 409) states that his analysis is not intended to explain the price and quantity combination chosen, but rather to explain why, once chosen, there will be no tendency to deviate from it. The price/quantity point chosen depends, in his words, 'upon the previous history of the case'. The concluding words of the Hall and Hitch study (1939, 125) are rather similar, for they state that to some extent the prices ruling at any time 'can only be explained in the light of the history of the industry'. However, as will now be demonstrated, a principal difference between the Sweezy and Hall-Hitch theories is that the latter not only attempts to explain price rigidity, but also, by invoking the full-cost doctrine, attempts to account for the level at which price is set.

3.3.   *The Contribution of Hall and Hitch*

It has been shown that Sweezy's version of the kinked demand curve is based first on the Kaldorian imagined demand curve and secondly on evidence that can be gathered by 'anyone who sets out to investigate the subject by interviewing businessmen'. In the version developed by Hall and Hitch, the theoretical underpinning is that introduced by Chamberlin (1933) in his *Theory of Monopolistic Competition*, and the empirical basis is provided by a report on the pricing policies of thirty-eight entrepreneurs, mainly in manufacturing business. An additional element in the Hall and Hitch theory is the introduction of the full-cost doctrine to explain the level at which price is set.

The relationship between kinked demand curves and the analysis of dd' and DD' curves introduced by Chamberlin (1933, ch. v) was dealt with in a purely technical sense in section 2.2 above. Figure 3.1 elaborates on that argument, and is a modified version of the original diagram contained in Hall and Hitch (1939, 117), which, as Welham (1973) shows, was sketched with rather implausible-looking average and marginal relationships. The curve dAD' is what was described in chapter 2 as an obtuse kink. It will be recalled that the dd' curve in Chamberlin's analysis shows the increase (decrease) in sales that a monopolistic competitor would experience by cutting (increasing) his price, given that other competitors hold theirs constant. The DD' curve shows the sales that will be realised by a single seller, given that the prices of other sellers are the same as his. This latter curve is

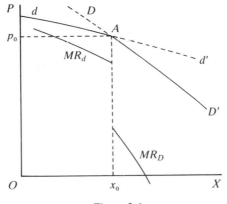

Figure 3.1

therefore $(1/n)$th of market demand at any given price, in the case of n sellers, given the Chamberlinian assumption of a uniform distribution of tastes over the product varieties.

The kinked demand curve of Hall and Hitch is dAD', with MR_d and MR_D being the corresponding marginal revenue curves. They produce the usual argument for price stability in the face of shifts in marginal cost, and also explore more explicitly than Sweezy the circumstances under which demand shifts will leave price unaffected. In figure 3.2 the changes in the relative elasticities of the upper and lower segments of the demand curve are illustrated for various demand shifts. AC is the short run average

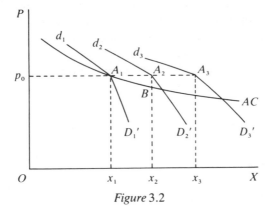

Figure 3.2

33

cost curve, excluding profits. As demand increases, and the firm operates at higher output levels, the upper segment becomes less elastic and the lower segment less inelastic. Hall and Hitch argue that price is set at p_0 according to a full-cost policy. A majority of firms in their sample set the product price by taking unit direct cost as a base, adding to that a percentage margin to cover indirect cost, and finally adding a further margin, which they frequently found to be 10 per cent, for profit.[1] In figure 3.2, it is supposed that at output level x_2 profits are what they were expected to be, being accounted for by a mark-up A_2B over an average cost of Bx_2. Provided the curve that is marginal to AC continues to cut the discontinuities pertaining to the marginal revenue curves of $d_1A_1D_1'$, $d_2A_2D_2'$ and $d_3A_3D_3'$, the price p_0 will continue to be optimal according to the criterion given in chapter 2. However, as Efroymson (1943) points out, the full-cost principle is apparently abandoned at output levels x_1 and x_3, for at x_1 the profit margin is zero, and at x_3 the profit margin exceeds the conventional magnitude BA_2 that is established by what Hall and Hitch (1939, 120) call 'the community of outlook of business men'.

In truth, as table 8 of their study suggests, there is a variety of circumstances under which the full-cost policy might be relaxed. In very depressed business conditions, or in very buoyant business conditions, price will tend to fall and to rise, respectively. In the latter case, Hall and Hitch argue, anticipating Efroymson (1943, 1955), the kinked demand curve will tend to be ironed out. Clearly the argument of Hall and Hitch is not as much at variance with the marginal analysis as the authors suggest. An obvious motive for holding price constant is to avoid adjustment costs. But more persuasive than this is that a price based on full cost need not be altered by a profit maximiser for a range of cost and demand shifts, provided the basic optimality condition of

1. Lest the reader be misled, it should be pointed out that there is no necessary connection between the kinked demand curve analysis and the full-cost principle – as is indeed evident from Sweezy's analysis. The full-cost principle is simply an *ex ante* method of fixing price in relation to an estimated level of demand. It is examined here because it has often been considered in tandem with a kinked short-run demand function for the individual firm, especially by P. W. S. Andrews, as in, for example, Andrews and Brunner (1975, ch. 2).

(2.5) above is satisfied. Further details of this range will be given in chapter 4. For cost or demand shifts outside this range, the full-cost policy will be modified, which again is in accordance with marginalist principles.

3.4. *Critics of Hall and Hitch*

It has already been hinted towards the end of the previous section that the original versions of the kinked demand curve theory did not stand uncriticised. Of the two works, that of Sweezy came in for far less criticism, possibly because it claimed less than the Hall-Hitch version, but perhaps also because no corroborating evidence was given at the time by Sweezy, but what proved to be a fairly easy target in terms of supporting evidence *was* given by Hall and Hitch. What might be termed the 'Cambridge critics', namely Professors Austin Robinson (1939) and Richard Kahn (1952), were mainly concerned with deficiencies in the technique of investigation employed by Hall and Hitch, though they were not exclusive in having made such points. Machlup (1946, 1952) developed a much more detailed critique of what he perceived to be an assault on the principle of marginalism. The major interpreter of the kinked demand curve theory, Clarence Efroymson, is a critic as well as an advocate.

Put briefly, Efroymson's (1943) criticism is that Hall and Hitch went both too far and not far enough. They went too far, for, as has been demonstrated in the previous section, there is a contradiction between the full-cost principle and the notion that price will be invariant under demand shifts. They did not go far enough, for they failed to push to its logical conclusion the consequences of their discussion about the variation of the elasticities of the upper and lower segments of the kinked demand curve with fluctuations in business conditions. Amongst the factors Efroymson sees as fostering the obtuse kink are caution and excess capacity. With a return to prosperity, caution is likely to be thrown to the wind, and excess capacity will disappear as a sellers' market emerges. This will tend to make the reversed, or reflex, kink illustrated in figure 2.1(d) emerge, with, as we shall see in chapter 4, quite different consequences for price setting. Price will tend to be unstable rather than rigidly fixed under these circumstances.

Robinson (1939) and Kahn (1952) (who covers much the same ground) are dubious about the conclusions of Hall and Hitch mainly because of the rather unsophisticated way in which the questionnaire was designed and the interviews were carried out. Robinson wishes that the status of the respondents had been reported (manager, accountant, etc.), and that the questionnaire itself had been published. These criticisms are very telling, and fortunately later efforts along these lines to investigate, amongst other things, the kinked demand curve have been more satisfactory. Studies from Shackle (1955) to Nowotny and Walther (1978), as reported in chapter 5, represent a continuous improvement in survey methods. Robinson is also critical of the lack of attention paid to the time period under consideration. Without reference to the price-fixing period the meaning of marginal cost is unclear, for much of what would conveniently be described as an overhead cost should more properly be described as a variable cost for a period as long as a year. On the demand side too, elasticity depends on the time period being considered, and in the very short run the meaning of a demand curve in itself becomes equivocal. These points are important, though somewhat loosely expressed, for they draw attention to the time dimension that should in strict logic appear when one discusses adjustment along the kinked demand curve. Stigler (1947), and Smith and Neale (1971), have given some attention to adjustments of the kinked demand curve period by period, but only Shubik (1959, 149) has seen clearly that the kinked demand curve is a concept *in time*, saying: 'The kinky oligopoly demand curve describes a time path through the contingent demand space'. The final point that Robinson makes is that the full-cost doctrine is simplistic in its neglect of anticipations. He argues, for example, that it might not be true that firms believe they will retain good-will by cutting prices. It is possible, he maintains, for a firm to anticipate that it will reinforce good-will by steadfastly refusing to cut price even in bad times, thus suggesting to customers that the good was always priced at the lowest level possible. Kahn (1952) elaborates and clarifies some of the criticism previously made by Robinson, but without substantially modifying the points already made, and also, more relevantly, deals explicitly with the kinked demand curve. He voices the familiar complaint that the kinked demand curve only explains why price remains where it is, arguing that the more interesting and important question is why price changes when it does, and the extent to which it changes. If what Kahn (1937) had earlier called *first-degree collusion* breaks down, very often through a general change in costs, then price will be revised. First-degree collusion depends on the notion that each firm holds the belief that a cut in his price would force the competitors to cut their prices, leading to a situation in which all are worse off. As Stigler (1978) has indicated, this behaviour precisely describes that underlying the lower branch of the kink. Even if first-degree collusion breaks down, price movements in the upward direction are moderated by the fear of new entry, and price cuts are limited because of *second-degree collusion.* Under this form of collusion, it is to the advantage of a firm in a group to cut price, but it does not do so because of a sense of affiliation. Fellner (1949, 43) has elsewhere called this *esprit de corps*, and in chapter 1 a similar reason advanced by Galbraith for price stability was discussed. As will be continually emphasised, there is no reason why a unique cause of price rigidity should exist. In fact Kahn regards the kinked demand curve explanation of price rigidity as subsidiary to his own explanation, which runs in terms of degree of collusion. Ultimately, the issue of which cause is most important is an empirical one, and there is no *prima facie* case for preferring one logically consistent explanation to another. To Kahn, the kinked demand curve theory is compatible with profit maximisation suitably modified to lie within an oligopoly framework. That this is true was made clear in chapter 2, where it was shown that the necessary modification simply entailed a 'peaked', rather than a 'smooth' maximum on the profit function.

Machlup (1946, 1952) has turned the heaviest guns on Hall and Hitch, but his argument is not really with the kinked demand curve analysis, which he reproduces with qualified approval in the second-named work, but with the full-cost doctrine, and perhaps more generally with 'direct empirical evidence'. History has ultimately proved the value of the methods handled, perhaps clumsily, by Hall and Hitch, and analysis confirms that there is no conflict between the kinked demand curve theory and marginalism.

3.5. *Conclusion*

In chapter 1, the kinked demand curve was introduced in a purely mechanical sense, and in chapter 2 the analytics of the curve were examined, shorn of interpretative details. However, forerunners such as Hayes (1928) and Robinson (1933) did not use the kinked demand curve to produce a durable theory: rather it was the rationale for the kink developed by Hall, Hitch and Sweezy that proved to have survival value. Their geometry resembles that of Hayes and Robinson, but here the resemblance ends, for Hall, Hitch and Sweezy were presenting a new theory: a theory that was aimed at explaining price rigidity in oligopolistic markets. Further, Hall and Hitch were trying to establish the efficacy of a new method of enquiry, involving the collection of direct empirical evidence on business behaviour.

It has been shown that the analytical bases of the Hall and Hitch and the Sweezy theories are different, the former being based on Chamberlin's dd' and DD' curves, and the latter on Kaldor's imagined demand curve. Today, by a custom which was very rapidly established, the two versions of the theory are fused, with an attendant loss of subtlety in design. The concern of the next chapter is with the literature that has grown out of this fusion of ideas.

4

Developments of the Theory

4.1. *Introduction*

Earlier chapters have examined the first analytical formulations of the kinked demand curve theory, and a few of the logical consequences of the theory have been explored. The purpose of this chapter is to consider in some detail theoretical developments of the kinked demand curve analysis. Over a hundred papers have been written on the topic, many making only very modest extensions, as Stigler (1978) has observed. Though many minor works will be referred to in this chapter, attention will be concentrated on the most significant contributions. The general thrust of the argument will be that the kinked demand curve analysis, though of a certain analytical interest in its own right, assumes greater importance in analytical terms when viewed as a theory that can be generalised to a broader, more fruitful, theory of contingent demand curves.

4.2. *Determinacy of the Analysis*

A common problem in the theory of the firm is what experts call 'oligopolistic indeterminacy'. In the theory of monopoly, or in the theory of perfect competition, key variables such as price, output and profit are determined by the interaction of the technical conditions of production and the subjective preferences of consumers. By contrast, in the theory of oligopoly, which is concerned with cases in which a few sellers are significantly interdependent, various forms of indeterminacy emerge, depending on the particular model under consideration. That is, the sort of information that is adequate to determine key variables for monopoly and perfect competition is no longer adequate for oligopoly. As the kinked demand curve theory purports to be a theory of oligopoly, it is clear that the problem of determinacy must be broached.[1]

Chapter 3 has already provided a foretaste of this issue, for there Kaldor's criticism that the demand curves used in *The Economics of Imperfect Competition* are indeterminate was mentioned. Furthermore, the argument that the price at which the kink occurs could be rendered determinate by invoking the full-cost principle was shown to be faulty. It will prove convenient in this section to consider determinacy under two headings suggested by our previous discussion. First, the determinacy of the demand curve itself will be explored. Secondly, and more briefly, the narrower issue of whether the price at which the kink occurs is determined within the framework of analysis, or is given exogenously by the history of the market, will be explored.

Joan Robinson (1933, 21) attempts to define the demand curve of the firm subject to imperfect competition in the following words: 'the demand curve for the individual firm may be conceived to show the full effect upon the sales of that firm which results from any change in the price which it charges, whether it causes a change in the price charged by the others or not'. Kaldor (1934) argues that such a demand curve is indeterminate, and substitutes for it an imagined demand curve. The latter curve, which has already been discussed in more detail in chapter 3, generally only coincides with the real demand curve at the point of equilibrium. Certainly Joan Robinson's analysis is unsatisfactory, and she seems unaware that (if indeterminacy is to be avoided) explicit consideration must be given to whether or not a rival changes price in response to any initiating price change. Ott (1962), following on from earlier work of Stackelberg, develops a full taxonomy of the assumptions that might be made about the prices and outputs of rivals, and includes within this taxonomy the assumptions underlying the obtuse kinked demand curve of Sweezy, Hall and Hitch, and the reflex kink of Efroymson. Chamberlin, with his device of DD' and dd' curves, attempts to grapple with the indeterminacy of the demand curve by adopting the two polar assumptions that either all rivals' prices follow a

---

1. It is worth emphasising that indeterminacy is a failure of theory alone, for in the real world events are determinate.

price change, or none at all. Joan Robinson does not really come to terms with the problem, and indeed in more recent years has repudiated her own analysis. Kaldor certainly recognises the problem, but sees it as insoluble, and cuts the Gordian knot by introducing a determinate imagined demand curve. However, one is left with the uneasy feeling that this line of argument, though it expedites matters greatly, really replaces a problem by a name. Although Kaldor would argue that people can hold expectations with certainty, is it not equally possible that some people might be *undecided,* or that yet others might think in terms of *ranges* of possible outcomes? Ultimately more satisfactory, it will be argued in this chapter, is to attempt to discover the objective outcomes, even be they great in number, which are possible under oligopoly. In section 4.6 below, a method for doing this, which runs in terms of contingent demand curves, is discussed. As the analysis of this topic by Machlup (1952) suggests, the way in which determinacy is achieved is by the introduction of additional variables.

An important but neglected argument, much emphasised by Andrews (1949, 1964), is that the demand curve in itself is indeterminate, for costs and demand are not independent. Efroymson (1943, 1955) develops the implications of such a position for the kinked demand curve, although there is no direct evidence of a link between his and Andrews's thought. Efroymson claims that the form of the kink depends on the degree of capacity utilisation. It would not be meaningful, therefore, to draw a kinked demand curve without reference to the conditions of production: without such a reference it is indeterminate. The basic analytics of Efroymson's argument have already been presented in chapter 2, but the rationale remains to be explained. Efroymson argues that the conventional kinked demand curve (or 'obtuse kink', in his words) is likely to be a feature of firms in an industry characterised by excess capacity. He finds it significant that Hall and Hitch undertook their investigations of prices policies in the years preceding 1937, for this would tend to bias business opinion to caution and pessimism.[1] However, if business conditions improve, then the pessimistic expectations embodied

---

1. It should be noted that even so, there was at this time considerable prosperity in some industries and in some areas.

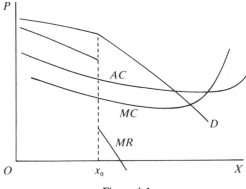

Figure 4.1

in the kink will be revised, and Efroymson is of the view that this process is rather rapid. At, or close to, capacity (which is identified with minimum average cost), this revision of expectations will cause the kink to reverse and become a 'reflex kink'. This argument is really a logical extension of the views of Hall, Hitch and Sweezy on the effect that improved business conditions would have on the elasticities of the two branches of the kink. However, in Sweezy's analysis, the average cost curve is never explicitly considered, and although it *is* by Hall and Hitch, the sellers' market case is not emphasised. In a sellers' market, in which all production is taking place at, or near, full capacity, firms may not be at all reluctant to follow price increases: indeed if unit costs are rapidly rising, they may welcome any opportunity to increase price. In this situation, a price cut will appear unattractive. The sight of a rival cutting his price may not induce a firm to follow suit. It may reason that the rival, like itself, is so close to capacity that it could not meet an increase in orders. This being the case, by following the price cut the firm would only find itself cutting revenue in the face of sharply rising costs, to the detriment of profit. In figure 4.1 the obtuse kinked demand curve (*D*) of Hall, Hitch and Sweezy is presented, along with the corresponding marginal revenue curve (*MR*). The average cost curve (*AC*) is drawn in a somewhat elongated form, a shape which is not inconsistent with empirical evidence, and the corresponding marginal cost curve (*MC*) is also shown. The form of the

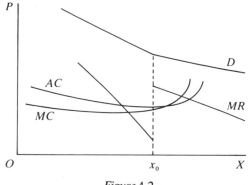

Figure 4.2

cost curve draws particular attention to the 'capacity' point, this
being at minimum average cost, where the MC curve cuts the AC
curve from below. The level of output chosen is x_0, which is well
below capacity. The kinked demand curve, in isolation from
cost, is indeterminate under this interpretation. A crude simplifi-
cation would be to regard a distinct kinked demand curve as
existing for each possible choice of x_0. In fact, the story is really
more complex than this, and cannot be accurately captured
(though its meaning can be suggested) by a two-dimensional
diagram. It has already been suggested that any oligopoly model
depends upon the assumptions that are made about the firms'
state of knowledge. Competition is not anonymous. The identity
of actual, and possibly even potential, rivals is known, and some
of their characteristics are understood, either through a volun-
tary exchange of information or by a mixture of surmise and such
information as is obtained by luck or guile. Thus firms are par-
tially but not wholly ignorant. Expectations are based on incomplete information, but information nevertheless. In the present
case it is assumed that the below-capacity output x_0 is taken as a
signal by the firm that rivals are likewise operating below capacity. There will thus be a mutual reinforcement of the pessimistic
expectations implied by the obtuse kink.

The sellers' market case of Efroymson is illustrated in figure
4.2. The output level x_0, so close to capacity, induces a switch of
the kinked demand curve from an obtuse to a reflex form. The

43

marginal cost curve cuts the marginal revenue curve at two points, to the right and left of the output at which the kink occurs. Either may define a global maximum for profit, and a criterion for determining which was given in chapter 2. The significant point is that x_0 cannot be an optimal choice of output. Therefore the situation illustrated in figure 4.2, unlike that in figure 4.1, represents an unstable price-output decision. Efroymson suggests that what will happen is that there will be a series of erratic movements between the various maxima. When one is reached, the operation of the reflex kink will cause local maxima to be set up again on either side of the newly chosen level of output. One of these will again be approached, and so this process will continue, with associated price and output fluctuations, until the profit maximising output is pushed to a level that is sufficiently below capacity that the oligopolist, believing other firms are in much the same situation as well, will suddenly revise his expectations to the pessimistic type implied by the obtuse kink. This extension of the scope of the kinked demand curve to sellers' markets will prove very useful for the interpretation of empirical evidence in chapter 5.

Although Efroymson is a notable critic of the unadorned kinked demand curve theory, what he does *not* dispute – and here he is joined by many others, including Sweezy (1939), Stigler (1947), and Kahn (1952) – is that the price at which the kink occurs is indeterminate. Indeed, this could be said to be one of the most popularly held views of the kinked demand curve analysis. However, Hawkins (1971) has argued that the location of the kink is determinate, and provides a construction by which it can be discovered.[1] He considers the case of small group competition where producers have similar cost and revenue functions of which they have objective knowledge. The lower section of the kinked demand curve is the lower part of Chamberlin's DD' curve, as described in chapters 2 and 3. The upper section of the kinked demand curve is part of Chamberlin's dd' curve, and must lie below the upper part of the DD' curve. Let the industry profit maximising price be P_m. Would it be rational for a price

1. It is not altogether settled that Hawkins's theorising is legitimate, involving as it does both traditional equilibrium theory with no history, and a process of adjustment from a given price.

greater than this to be established (say P_0) further up along the DD' curve, with the dd' curve meeting it at P_0 to establish the kink? Evidently not, because the firm should reduce price in order to increase profit, for marginal cost will not go through the gap in the marginal revenue curve, but through the lower branch. There will continue to be an incentive to cut price, even though rivals may follow (as they must, by the DD' curve construction), until price has reached P_m. By converse reasoning, it is readily established that price should not be less than P_m. That is, the location of the kink is determinate, and rests at the industry's profit maximising price. Should costs fall, then this price P_m will also fall, implying downward flexibility of prices; but should costs rise, price will not rise until marginal cost has risen beyond the gap in the marginal revenue curve. In the latter case, rising costs imply an upward rigidity of prices, and this weakens the determinacy of the kink. It is now only known that the kink must lie on the DD' curve at a price that is less than or equal to the profit maximising price for the industry. However, it should be noted that Hawkins's analysis is applied for the homogeneous case, in which all costs and revenues are identical and known with certainty. If costs and revenues differ, such a straightforward analysis cannot be expected to emerge. There is no *prima facie* case for supposing that the indeterminacy of the kink cannot be removed in more complicated cases, but clearly an appropriate analysis would be more complex, and, as is a general rule if indeterminacy is to be banished, would involve the introduction of further objective information. In section 4.6 it will be shown how such additional information can be used to generate objectively defined contingent demand curves with objectively defined kinks. If firms maximise profits, given such curves, the tendency is for the optimal price to be located at a kink, because of the peakedness a kink tends to induce in the profit function. Should this be the case, then both the demand curve and the location of the kink should be regarded as determinate.

4.3.   *Comparative Statics Properties*

The method of comparative statics is employed to investigate the change in a model from one position of equilibrium to another, without enquiring into the path by which the change was accomplished. The comparative statics properties of the kinked demand curve are very well known, barring details, and indeed at a number of points it has already been implicitly assumed that the reader has some passing acquaintance with them. It is now the place to give these properties the treatment that is due to them, both for the sake of completeness, and in order to tidy up some logical niceties that are sometimes glossed over.

Neither Hall and Hitch (1939) nor Sweezy (1939) make great play of the comparative statics properties of the model, though it is true to say, contrary to the assertion of Bronfenbrenner (1940), that the analysis is present in their works. Sweezy (1939, 406) talks of shifts in the position of the marginal cost curve that will leave the equilibrium price and output unaffected. He also discusses shifts in demand that, with the resulting change in the elasticities of the upper and lower branches of the kinked demand curve, will alter the length of discontinuity in the marginal revenue curve, and hence the range of cost variation over which price will be held constant. Hall and Hitch (1939, 117) are aware that for any marginal cost curve that goes through the discontinuity in the marginal revenue curve, the profit maximising price will be unaltered. At another point they examine the consequences of demand shifts along the lines already demonstrated in chapter 3. However, neither treatment is systematic, and although at one point readers of Sweezy are encouraged to experiment for themselves with pencil and paper, the workaday but doubtless necessary task of developing a systematic treatment of comparative statics has been accomplished by Bronfenbrenner (1940). Notably good treatments of comparative statics, along similar lines, are in Lange (1944, ch. 7) and Machlup (1952, ch. 14), and textbook developments, of varying degrees of accuracy, are numberless.

In figure 4.3 the consequences of various marginal cost shifts are examined. Two extreme cases are illustrated, with marginal cost MC_1 at the lower end N and with MC_2 at the upper end K of the gap (KN) in the marginal revenue curve (MR). Any marginal cost variation within this gap will leave the equilibrium price and quantity unaltered[1] at p_0 and x_0. A movement upwards of mar-

1. Bronfenbrenner (1940, 423) suggests that a suitable measure of 'oligopoly cost price rigidity' is $2(p_2 - p_1)/(p_2 + p_1)$.

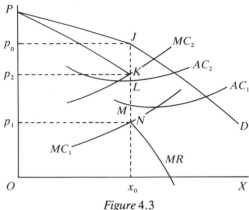

Figure 4.3

ginal cost from MC_1 to MC_2 entails a reduction of the degree of monopoly from JN/Jx_0 to JK/Jx_0. Further, the unit profit is reduced from JM to JL, and as a consequence (for equilibrium output is still x_0), total profit is also reduced. This consideration leads Sweezy (1939, 406) to argue that there is more than a grain of truth in the trade union argument that higher wages, with the consequential upward pressure on average and marginal costs, will only reduce profit, but not increase the product price. However, as Machlup (1952, 473) points out, this argument is subject to a fallacy of composition if any attempt is made to generalise it to the level of the industry. If all firms are subject to such cost increases, and each firm is aware that this is happening to its rivals, there will be a bodily upward shift of the kinked demand curve, and the selling price for all firms will be raised. This is a plausible argument, given the contingent demand curve analysis of section 4.6 below, but actually is not well founded on the view that the price level at which the kink occurs is indeterminate or given by 'previous history'.

The comparative statics of demand shifts is somewhat more complex, but the simplest version will be considered first. Bronfenbrenner (1940, 422) considers the case in which parallel shifts of the upper and lower segments of the kinked demand curve occur. This is illustrated in figure 4.4 by the shift from D_1 to D_2 with the consequential shifts of the discontinuous marginal revenue curves from MR_1 to MR_2. For the given marginal cost curve

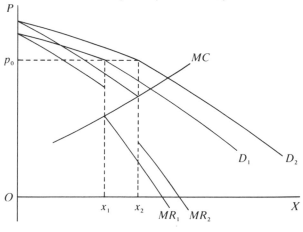

Figure 4.4

MC, the shift from D_1 to D_2 is the greatest that can take place without the equilibrium price p_0 being affected. This range of demand price rigidity is narrower than that suggested by Bronfenbrenner, because he tacitly assumes that the gap in the marginal revenue curve is uninfluenced by the parallel demand shift. In fact, as Smith (1948) points out, the gap narrows for a demand contraction, and increases for a demand expansion. This is because for a given leftward parallel shift of a linear demand curve, the marginal revenue curve must shift parallel and leftwards by only half as much. Suitably corrected, Bronfenbrenner's coefficient of 'demand price rigidity' is given by $2(x_2 - x_1)/(x_2 + x_1)$. As a general measure of oligopolistic price rigidity he suggests the arithmetic mean of his two coefficients.

In fact both Hall and Hitch (1939) and Sweezy (1939) do not consider the case of parallel shifts in the kinked demand curve as at all plausible. They argue that as demand grows the upper branch will become less elastic, and the lower branch more elastic. This will tend to iron out the kink, and therefore, to diminish the discontinuity in the marginal revenue curve. This effect, the narrowing of the gap as demand expands, is in fact contrary to the Bronfenbrenner construction. Its consequence is a narrowing of the range of marginal cost variation, which will make for rigid prices, and given the presumption that marginal

48

cost is likely to be moving up as demand is expanding, it suggests that a price increase, rather than cut, is likely to be associated with a demand increase. In the converse case, of a demand contraction, the gap in the marginal revenue curve will enlarge as the upper branch of the kinked demand curve becomes more elastic, and the lower branch less elastic. This will increase the tendency to price rigidity, given the likely downward pressure on costs as demand falls. Indeed, in the extreme case that the elasticity of demand for price reductions is less than one, there is no marginal cost reduction that could reduce the equilibrium price. In this case, the discontinuity in the marginal revenue curve is so great that marginal revenue for the lower branch of the kink is everywhere negative. This is the case illustrated by Sweezy (1939, 405), and may have been the extreme case that Gardiner Means (1935) had in mind in his own discussion of price rigidity.

So far, discussion has concentrated on cases in which shifts of demand and cost have been such that no revision of the equilibrium price and quantity (p_0 and x_0) has been necessary. Smith and Neale (1972) provide a detailed, indeed intricate, analysis of demand shifts that bring about an intersection of the marginal cost and marginal revenue curves outside the discontinuity in the marginal revenue curve. Their starting point is the DD', dd' curve version of the kinked demand curve. The analysis recognises four basic categories of individuals: optimists, who prefer to move along the DD' curve, and have their expectations confirmed; pessimists, who prefer to move along the dd' curve, and have their expectations confirmed; optimists who have their expectations controverted and become pessimists, ultimately preferring adjustment along the dd' curve; and pessimists who have their expectations controverted and become optimists, ultimately preferring adjustment along the DD' curve. Two other, less plausible categories, of optimists and pessimists who are always proved wrong, but never change, are also discussed. It is shown that in each case, adjustments will be made from an out-of-equilibrium position to a new equilibrium in which marginal cost cuts the upper or lower end of the gap in the marginal revenue curve. The fastest adjustment occurs (in just one step) if the views of optimists or pessimists are confirmed. A longer

49

period of adjustment is necessary if expectations are incorrect, but Smith and Neale show that convergence to a new equilibrium will still occur. The direction of the demand shift is a critical part of the analysis and a hysteresis type of result is demonstrated. Consider two kinked demand curves D_1 and D_2. If the movement of demand is from D_1 to D_2 the consequential price increase is greater than the consequential price decrease if the movement of demand is from D_2 to D_1. The analysis is ingenious, and, running as it does in terms of revisions of expectations, is much more satisfactory than any mechanical application of comparative statics methods. However, the convergence results are only derived for parallel movements in the segments of the kinked demand curve. It remains to be seen whether they are preserved if the elasticities of the segments vary as the kinked demand curve shifts.

4.4. *Supply Kinks*

Although the kinked demand curve analysis was devised to illuminate certain aspects of product market behaviour, there is no reason why analogous arguments should not apply to the factor market. It has already been suggested in chapter 2 that kinks might appear in the average cost function, with the consequence that the marginal cost function has a discontinuity. However, no clear rationale for this was developed. The purpose of this section is to provide a fuller analysis of supply kinks.

Commentators on the kinked demand curve analysis, such as Bronfenbrenner (1940), Stigler (1947) and Lange (1944), very quickly realised that just as there could be asymmetries in the sellers' market, so there could be in the buyers' market. The theory of *oligopsony* is concerned with those factor markets in which there are few buyers, and where therefore each buyer will be conscious that his own purchasing policy will interact with his rivals' purchasing policies.

It will be recalled that in the case of monopsony, a single buyer faces a rising market supply curve for each factor. If the monopsonist sells in a perfectly competitive market, profit maximisation requires that the marginal cost of the factor is set equal to the value of its marginal product. If the monopsonist is also a monopolist in the product market, profit maximisation requires that the marginal revenue product of the factor is set equal to its marginal cost. The terminology is not firmly established for such models, and it is common to find the average cost and marginal cost of a factor referred to as the *average factor outlay* and the *marginal factor outlay* respectively. This is the practice that will be followed in this section. It will generally be assumed that there is some degree of imperfection in the product market, and hence the marginal product curve referred to will be the marginal revenue product curve.

By analogy with monopsony-monopoly, under oligopsony-monopoly or oligopsony-oligopoly, with smooth functions, profit maximisation requires that the marginal revenue product be set equal to the marginal factor outlay. If the marginal curves exhibit discontinuities, then this condition must be modified, along the lines indicated in chapter 2, to the condition that for an amount employed of the factor which is less than optimal, the marginal revenue product must exceed the marginal factor outlay, and for an amount employed of the factor which exceeds the optimal, the marginal factor outlay must exceed the marginal revenue product.

Bronfenbrenner (1940, 426–77) was the first to investigate the possibility that the factor supply curve of the oligopsonist might be kinked. He, like all other writers on this topic, emphasises the case in which the factor under consideration is labour, although this is not a necessary interpretation. The diagram to be used in illustrating the supply kink will continue to be drawn between P and X axes, although it will prove convenient on occasion to regard X as the amount of labour and P as the wage. It will be supposed in the first instance that there is no control over factor supply, implying that if the factor is regarded as labour, the case of organised, or unionised, labour is ruled out. In figure 4.5 the price paid for the factor is p_0. If the interpretation given to p_0 by all writers on the topic is to be followed, this price should be regarded as given by historical circumstances. It is argued that if an oligopsonist raises price above p_0 his rivals will tend to match him, for fear of losing supply. If price is reduced below p_0, suppliers will rapidly shift to other buyers. Thus the factor supply curve (or, equivalently, the average factor outlay curve, AFO) has a kink at p_0, being more elastic below this price than above. It

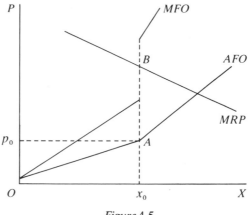

Figure 4.5

has been known at least since Robinson (1933) that the corresponding marginal curve has the discontinuous form of the marginal factor outlay curve (*MFO*) given in figure 4.5.

This discontinuity in the *MFO* curve implies, by reasoning similar to that employed in section 4.3 above, that the price p_0 will tend to be unresponsive to shifts in the marginal revenue product curve, and to certain classes of shift in factor supply (i.e. shifts of the *AFO* curve). By analogy with the degree of monopoly defined in chapter 2, a *degree of monopsony* may be defined, as Lange (1944, 41) suggests, for the oligopsony case, it being the ratio of the excess of marginal revenue product over price, to the price. Thus in figure 4.5 it is given by the ratio BA/Ax_0. The effect of an expansion of demand is generally to leave price and output unchanged at p_0 and x_0, and therefore to increase the degree of monopsony. Coyne (1975, 145) uses such an argument to explain the observed phenomenon of labour hoarding. As demand increases the surplus going to the oligopsonist increases,[1] but hiring remains constant. If demand should subsequently fall, provided the *MRP* curve shifts down within the range of discontinuity in the *MFO* curve, the expected 'shake-out' of labour predicted by conventional theory does not occur, that is, labour is hoarded. The only factor market adjustment that takes place is

1. And so also does the product price increase, assuming no kinked demand in the product market.

that the degree of monopsony is diminished.

The existence of a kinked *AFO* curve with a corresponding discontinuity in *MFO* implies that the oligopsonist-oligopolist will have a kinked marginal cost curve, as illustrated in chapter 2. This kink will occur at the optimal output level as well, because it results from a kink in the *AFO* curve at exactly that level of factor usage that is required to produce the optimal output. The existence of discontinuities in both the marginal cost and marginal revenue curves will exacerbate the tendency to price rigidity.

Coyne (1975), who has written the most complete account of supply kinks, attempts to extend the analysis to the case of organised labour, in which a monopolistic seller of làbour (the union) faces an oligoposonistic group of buyers of labour services. It is already known that a monopoly-monopsony analysis of such a situation is indeterminate, and it therefore comes as no surprise that Coyne's analysis of monopoly-oligopsony reveals even more severe problems of indeterminacy.

4.5.   *Doubly Kinked Demand Curves*

It has been shown that the kinked demand curve may assume a variety of shapes, depending on the elasticities of the upper and lower segments. Cecchella (1975) and Stigler (1978) mention many types of kinked demand curves that do not have the Sweezy-Hall-Hitch interpretation, including those analysed by Hieser (1953), Grossack (1966) and Greenhut (1967). Unfortunately, most of these variants are too disparate in kind to be discussed in a systematic way.

However, one variant, the *doubly kinked demand curve*, is worthy of further attention. It is often mentioned in connection with the conventional kinked demand curve theory, and also leads discussion in a natural way towards the theory of contingent demand curves, which is to be developed in the next section. The curve was employed by Machlup (1952) in his analysis of imperfect monopoly, and has subsequently been adopted to an oligopoly context by Gutenberg (1955, 1965), Kilger (1962), Albach (1965, 1979), Willeke (1964), Brockhoff (1968) and Manzetti (1977).

Machlup (1952, 557–61) considers a monopolist who would be subject to competition if price were either too low or too high. If

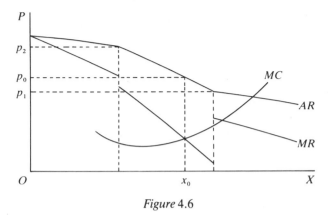

Figure 4.6

the price were raised too much, another commodity, which customers had previously never regarded as a substitute, would now be purchased. If the price were dropped down very low, the product might start to qualify for uses that would never have seemed sensible when it was highly priced. As a consequence, the demand curve becomes suddenly more elastic above and below a monopoly zone, giving it a 'doubly kinked' appearance. This is illustrated in figure 4.6. The doubly kinked demand curve is given by AR, with the kinks at prices p_2 and p_1 being of the form that Efroymson would describe as obtuse and reflex, respectively. The marginal revenue curve, MR, is made up of the three segments lying below the doubly kinked curve. In the case illustrated, the marginal cost curve, MC, cuts MR at two points, but, by the criterion given in chapter 2, the optimal output is x_0, implying an optimal price of p_0, which lies in the monopoly zone.

This theory has been developed by Gutenberg (1955, 1965), for the case of oligopoly, although in its simplest form his analysis pertains to duopoly. Gutenberg argues that the duopolist's demand curve has a monopolistic section in the neighbourhood of its rival's price, and infinitely elastic sections at the extremes. He argues for the existence of the monopolistic region on the basis of five factors, including quality of market information and the reaction speed of buyers.[1] The pure form of his argument is

1. The term 'reaction speed' is something of a misnomer, for Gutenberg's analysis is not explicitly dynamic.

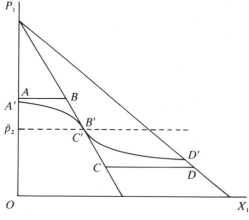

Figure 4.7

modified to recognise a less than infinite reaction speed, but one which increases the further price moves from the monopolistic region. In its application to oligopoly, the monopolistic region of the curve is centred around some average price, $\bar{p}$, for the group of competitors.

The case of duopoly can be explained by reference to figure 4.7. The curve through $D'D$ is the market demand curve, and $BB'C'C$ is a section of Firm 1's demand curve. In Gutenberg's simplest case Firm 1 has a demand curve given by $ABCD$. The equation for this curve is given by

$$p_1 = a - 2bx_1 + c(p_2 - p_1)$$

which is defined for any assigned value $(p = \bar{p}_2)$ of Firm 2's price. In this equation a and b are positive constants, and c is not a constant in the usual sense, but a peculiar parameter, which is zero provided the absolute deviation of p_1 from $\bar{p}_2$ is less than some assigned positive magnitude Δ, but tends to positive (negative) infinity if p_1 is less (greater) than $\bar{p}_2$ by an amount that exceeds Δ. Gutenberg discusses the behaviour of the parameter c in terms of the loyalty of customers. In the case being considered there is a sudden switch from loyalty to disloyalty. Along the stretch BC, customers of Firm 1 remain loyal. If p_1 reaches B, customers desert Firm 1, and if p_1 reaches C, customers desert

Firm 2. Along BC, $c = 0$, along AB, $c = -\infty$, and along CD, $c = \infty$. Gutenberg modifies this discussion of the pure case by suggesting that something like the curve $A'B'C'D'$ in figure 4.7 is more plausible than $ABCD$, implying a shorter range along the demand curve of total customer loyalty and a smoother transition from loyal to disloyal behaviour. Kilger (1962) explains the smoother doubly kinked demand curve in terms of a demand function with interaction terms. These interaction terms provide 'distance measures' between suppliers, and between the preferences of buyers. This work anticipates that of Shapley and Shubik (1969), which is to be discussed in the next section. Albach (1965) explains the doubly kinked demand curve in terms of the cost of switching between suppliers. These costs may be informational, or transactional, but can also be regarded as purely psychic, that is, as reflecting particular subjective preferences for one supplier over another. Given a price set by Firm 2, no capacity constraints, and identical costs of change for each customer, a doubly kinked demand curve like $ABCD$ in figure 4.7 emerges. However, a smoothed doubly kinked demand curve like $A'B'C'D'$ would emerge if the costs of changing suppliers varied between customers. Albach (1965, 19) also provides a functional form to approximate the curve $A'B'C'D'$, using a mixture of a linear and a hyperbolic function:

$$p_1 = a - 2bx_1 + c \sinh(p_2 - p_1)$$

In Albach (1979) a modified version of this function is estimated for a product in the German pharmaceuticals' market. Brockhoff (1968) has undertaken the trivial extension of permitting c to be negative, thus providing a functional form suitable for estimating a smoothed version of the plateau type demand function of Smith (1935). In a technically inaccurate paper, Manzetti (1977) attempts to explore the consequences of expansion or contraction of market demand for a doubly kinked demand curve along much the same lines as Efroymson did for the conventional kinked demand curve. He concludes that the equilibrium point tends to move up in expansion and down in contraction. However, the argument, which is developed for a sales revenue maximising firm, amounts to little more than the proposition that if demand becomes less (more) elastic as business conditions

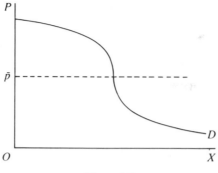

Figure 4.8

improve (deteriorate), price will tend to rise (fall).

To summarise, the doubly kinked demand curve that appears in the literature is usually one of the variants descended from the analysis of Gutenberg (1955). Figure 4.8 illustrates a typical synthesis of these various models. It illustrates the demand curve (D) for the product of a single producer operating in a market of heterogeneous oligopoly. The price $\bar{p}$, about which the less elastic part of the curve is centred, is the average of the prices charged by firms in this oligopolistic group. There are no kinks as such in the demand curve, these having been smoothed out because of varying degrees of customer loyalty, varying costs amongst purchasers of switching between suppliers, etc. The total revenue function for a demand curve of this type has a shape that resembles a cubic polynomial. When considered in conjunction with the cost curve, this generates a profit function that generally has multiple maxima. These may be dealt with analytically along the lines indicated in chapter 2.

4.6.   The Theory of Contingent Demand Curves

A number of writers, including Stigler (1947), Sweezy (1938), Efroymson (1943) and Gutenberg (1965) have realised that a complete analysis of the kinked demand curve involves considerations that are ignored, or dismissed as insignificant, in the theories of monopoly and of perfect competition. Sweezy, for example, is aware that inventory accumulation and decumulation should be considered. Amongst the factors that Stigler lists as affecting the kink are the relative size of rivals and the degree of product heterogeneity. Efroymson points out that the extent of capacity utilisation can affect the kink. Finally, as the last section has indicated, Gutenberg shows that to *each* price set by the rival (or to every average of the rivals' prices) a demand curve can be constructed, having a form that is influenced by such factors as the cost of switching suppliers and the degree of consumer loyalty. In the discussion of determinacy it was pointed out that very often a situation is perceived as indeterminate only because certain types of determining factors are excluded from the domain of discourse, perhaps because they are regarded as being 'non-economic' in character. However, all the factors mentioned above are distinctly economic in character, and yet have tended to be ignored by theorists attempting to extend traditional areas of the theory of the firm to oligopoly situations.

A theorist at whom this accusation could not be levelled is Martin Shubik (1959, 149), who is of the view that 'Sweezy and Stigler do not specify enough about the actual structure of the markets to which they wish to apply the kinky demand analysis. If they did, they would be able to justify their assumptions by demonstrating that the behaviour of the particular firms being examined was constrained by technological, financial, and corporate facts within very narrow bounds'. Aside from the misattribution of views to Stigler, the position of Shubik is persuasive, and involves taking *explicit* account of such factors as the capacity limitations of rivals, transport costs, and the degre of substitution between rivals' goods. A basic analytical device of Shubik's work is the *contingent demand function,* and something very like it has already been encountered in figure 4.7 above. The purpose of this section is to provide a development of this theory, and to show that the kinked demand curve is but one type of contingent demand curve.

A framework for the theory of contingent demand curves may be developed as follows. Suppose there are n firms selling a differentiated product. To simplify, consider the case of only $2n$ variables: n prices and n production rates. If quantity is the dependent variable, the contingent demand function of the ith firm may be written:

$$x_i = f_i(p_i | [x_j, p_j], i \neq j)$$

where $[x_j, p_j]$, $i \neq j$, is the set of outputs and prices for all but the ith firm. If price is the dependent variable, then the contingent demand function should be written in its inverse form as

$$p_i = F_i(x_i | [x_j, p_j], i \neq j)$$

For any given set of $2(n-1)$ production rates and prices a contingent demand function exists, which may be expressed either as f_i or F_i. These functions are defined, in general, in a $2n$-dimensional space, but once $2(n-1)$ variables are assigned, a two-dimensional relationship between p_i and x_i can be drawn. For every possible set of values of $[x_j, p_j]$, $i \neq j$, there is a contingent demand curve for the ith firm.

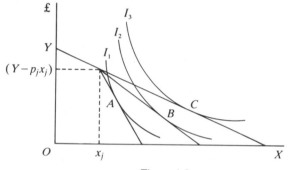

Figure 4.9

As an example of how a contingent demand curve may be constructed, consider the simple case illustrated in figure 4.9. This refers to the case in which a single buyer of a homogeneous good may buy from several suppliers, but in restricted quantities. The buyer is assumed to be a utility maximiser with a sum Y available for making purchases of the good. His preference function is represented by the indifference curves I_1, I_2, I_3. Suppose the consumer is considering purchasing from the ith or the jth supplier, and that $p_j < p_i$, implying the jth supplier will be approached first. However, it is assumed that $p_j x_j < Y$, implying that the restricted amount available, x_j, is not sufficient to satisfy the consumer's demand. The contingent demand function may

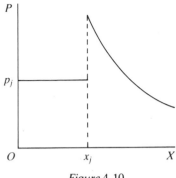

Figure 4.10

therefore be expressed as

$$x_i = f_i(p_i|x_j, p_j)$$

Figure 4.9 shows how it can be explicitly constructed. In the elementary case, in which each supplier offers an unlimited amount, the lowest price wins the business of the customer, and the demand curve is constructed by mapping the equilibrium points along the price consumption curve into the price-quantity space. A similar construction can still be employed in the present case, with the proviso that the consumer contemplating purchasing from the ith trader should now be regarded as having only $(Y-p_jx_j)$ available for purchases, part of his demand having already been satisfied at a lower price by the jth supplier. The budget constraint line is now rotated about the point $(x_j, Y-p_jx_j)$, rather than about (O, Y), and the demand curve is obtained by mapping tangency points such as A and B into the (x, p) space. Clearly for amounts purchased just greater than x_j, the demand price will be much higher than p_j. For greater amounts purchased this demand price will fall, until a point is eventually reached (C) at which $p_j=p_i$. For p_i less than p_j, the amount demanded can be obtained as in the elementary case, by rotating the budget line about the point (O, Y). Figure 4.10 illustrates the demand curve that results from following the procedure outlined above. The aggregate market demand function may be obtained, but not without further conceptual problems such as Shubik (1959, 85–7) indicates, by summing over

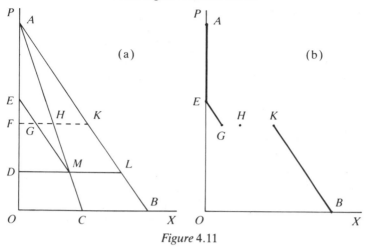

Figure 4.11

individual demand functions.

The jump in the demand curve shown in figure 4.10 is quite characteristic of contingent demand curves. They are rarely continuous convex curves, but may possess kinks, gaps and cusps. Some of these possible forms of contingent demand curves will now be considered in a more complicated context.

The development by Shapley and Shubik (1969) of a penetrating analysis of non-co-operative oligopoly with product differentiation and capacity constraints provides a suitable vehicle for a discussion of more complex forms of contingent demand curves. They develop their most complex analysis by building on a series of simpler cases. The first and second consider the production of a homogeneous good by two firms; and two sub-cases, with and without capacity constraints, are investigated. The third considers product differentiation without capacity constraint, and therefore has something in common with the analysis of Gutenberg (1955). The fourth considers differentiated duopoly with capacity constraints. Building on these foundations, Shapley and Shubik analyse the most complex case of differentiated oligopoly with capacity constraints.

It is postulated that an 'aggregate consumer' maximises a quadratic utility function, implying that aggregate demand is linear. Figures 4.11(a) and (b) illustrate the construction of the contingent demand curve when there are two firms producing a homogeneous good with, and without, capacity constraint. In figure 4.11(a), the line AB is the market demand function. AC is the demand curve for Firm 1, assuming Firm 2 charges the same price. It is closely related, logically speaking, to Chamberlin's DD' curve. The average cost is assumed to be constant at OD for both firms, and it is supposed initially that either firm could supply the entire market at any price. Suppose Firm 2 sets a price of OF. Then if Firm 1 also prices at OF, the market will be shared at point H. If Firm 1 prices above OF, it will sell nothing, implying its demand curve lies along AF. If it prices below OF, it will take all of the market from Firm 2, implying a demand curve below price OF of KB. Thus Firm 1's contingent demand curve, given that Firm 2 prices at OF, is given by segment AF, point H, and segment KB.

Suppose now that both firms have equal capacity and that at a price of OD the total output of the firms exactly satisfies market demand. If Firm 2 again sets a price of OF, Firm 1 will again share the market at H if it sets the same price. But if Firm 1 prices slightly above OF, it will find itself still able to supply FG, for the capacity limitation of Firm 2 prevents an amount greater than $GK\ (=ML=DM)$ being supplied. The segment EG, which is parallel to AB, indicates the demand for the product of Firm 1 if it prices above the level OF set by Firm 2. At and beyond OE, all the market goes to Firm 2. Below a price of OF, the demand for the product of Firm 1 lies along KB. In summary, the contingent demand curve for Firm 1, given that Firm 2 sets price at OF, and has capacity ML, is made up of segments AE, EG, point H, and segment KB. This construction has been used by Coase (1934), and is a close analytical relative of Chamberlin's dd' curve. For clarity, the contingent demand curve derived in this paragraph is separately illustrated in figure 4.11(b) by the thick black line.

Shapley and Shubik (1969) bring product differentiation into the argument by introducing an interaction factor of the form $\epsilon(x_1 - x_2)^2$ into the aggregate utility function, where ϵ is a parameter controlling the degree of product differentiation. They show that in this case the contingent demand curve for Firm 1 is as indicated by the thick line segments AB, BC and CD in figure 4.12(a). At point C, Firm 2 has been priced out of the market.

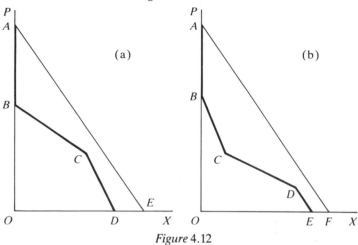

Figure 4.12

AE is the market demand curve, and the fact that the gap in demand of DE remains, even when Firm 1 prices close to zero, is a reflection of the lack of complete substitutability between the products of the two firms. There is no sudden switch from one supplier to another, as in the contingent demand curve in figure 4.11(b). Over the segment BC, which is defined for prices adjacent to the price set by Firm 2, there is a smooth transition from one product demand to the other, which is akin to that discussed in the previous section with respect to figure 4.7. If capacity constraints as well as product differentiation are introduced, then the contingent demand curve has the form $ABCDE$ indicated in figure 4.12(b). The effect of capacity constraint is to introduce the additional kink at C.

It has now been established that under differentiated oligopoly it is possible to construct demand curves that have various types of kinks by giving explicit consideration to capacity constraints and the degree of product differentiation. This has been shown to be possible even in the very simple cases considered, which neglect inventories, selling costs and inter-temporal effects. Shubik (1959, 149) argues that Sweezy's kinked demand curve is a dynamic demand curve that tells one that 'the demand faced by the i'th individual at time t is determined by the physical conditions (i.e. the contingent demand space) and the strategies of all the other firms'. This use of a simple curve to represent a complex dynamic demand relationship has analytical convenience to recommend it. A full analysis requires that for each firm every possible contingent demand function is calculated for every possible set of prices, outputs, advertising outlays, etc., of its rivals. If loss functions for inventories, and the cost curves of rivals are known, this information, in conjunction with knowledge of the contingent demand curves, enables payoffs to be objectively defined for every conceivable set of actions by the oligopolists. In this way, a full analysis of the kinked demand curve is conceptually possible. Of course, it is unlikely that it would have the simple form attributed to it by Hall, Hitch and Sweezy. Their analysis is but a sub-case of a more general theory of contingent demand curves.

4.7.   *Conclusion*

With the exception of the largely contemporary works to be discussed in chapter 6, all the main developments of the kinked demand curve theory have been examined in this chapter. A number of conventional extensions such as supply kinks, and comparative statics properties, have been treated, as well as less well known ones such as the doubly kinked demand curve. The issue of the determinacy of the analysis has been considered, and also the relationship of the kinked demand curve to contingent demand curves in general. The argument has been that the kinked demand curve theory, as currently expounded, is indeterminate largely because of an unnecessary exclusion of additional variables. These additional variables, such as the level of capacity and the cost of switching suppliers, can be incorporated in a contingent demand curve analysis that is fully determinate.

However, two issues have been neglected: the first being the role of information; and the second being the macroeconomic consequences of kinked supply and demand schedules. Concerning information, the tacit assumption behind the contingent demand curve analysis is that there is full knowledge of costs, capacity, inventories, and so on. The informational requirements for constructing contingent demand curves are therefore very great. In addition, a great deal of computation is required to derive a full set of contingent demand curves. Thus although the contingent demand curve theory is a great advance in that it extends the range of calculations that are conceptually possible, it makes no allowance for the frailties of economic agents. The theory of bounded rationality emphasises the limited capability for storage of information and computation that the human mind possesses, and a complete analysis of oligopoly must take cognisance of this factor.

The second neglected facet of the kinked demand curve theory in the preceding pages has been its macroeconomic consequences. This has been partly a result of the general orientation of this monograph towards microeconomics, but also because, with the signal exception of Lange (1944), few writers on the topic have pursued this matter. Lange in his *Price Flexibility and Employment* had developed the argument that oligopoly and oligopsony, with the consequential kinked product demand and labour supply curves, prevent the inter- and intra-temporal substitution that is necessary for the maintenance or restoration of general equilibrium. However, a preoccupation of economic theorists in the intervening years has been with a frictionless passage to general equilibrium. Only in the last few years has a concerted effort been made to understand the macroeconomic properties of an economy with a mixture of markets, some with flexible, and some with inflexible prices. The task of developing that theory to encompass kinked supply and demand functions is still in the process of being accomplished. Negishi (1979) has made progress in this direction using the device of a 'perceived demand curve', which is very close to Sweezy's 'imaginary demand curve', to investigate the consequences that kinked perceived demand curves have for Keynesian equilibrium. A perceived demand curve has the (inverse) form

$$p = p(x, \bar{p}, \bar{x})$$

where $\bar{p}$ and $\bar{x}$ are current price and current output in some initial position of the firm. This demand curve has the property that $\bar{p} = p(\bar{x}, \bar{p}, \bar{x})$ and that $p = \bar{p}$ for $x \leq \bar{x}$ and $\partial p / \partial x < 0$ for $x > \bar{x}$. Thus the perceived demand curve passes through the initial position, is infinitely elastic for outputs less than current sales, and is negatively sloped for outputs greater than current sales. In short, it is kinked at $(\bar{p}, \bar{x})$, the initial position. In a model of competitive firms possessing such perceived demand curves under conditions of demand deficiency, Negishi (1979, ch. 7) shows, for a given money wage, that price and output will remain unchanged even if price exceeds marginal cost. Under such circumstances, a marginal shift in demand will change output, but not price, thus providing an explanation of fixprice markets. A similar model is developed for labour-supplying households that may experience involuntary unemployment. In this case a kinked perceived demand curve implies that shifts in demand are absorbed by changes in the level of employment without the level of wages being affected. The existence of a Keynesian underemployment equilibrium is demonstrated for such a model.

The above argument suggests that there are two principal areas in which developments of the kinked demand curve theory should take place. The first is in that field which is concerned with imperfections of information, learning, and the formulation of expectations. The second is in the area of macroeconomics, where the consequences of rigidities in certain markets need to be explored more fully.

Developments of the Empirical Evidence

5.1. *Introduction*

In chapter 3, the early studies of Hall and Hitch (1939) and Sweezy (1939) were examined, and some of the criticisms of these early studies were considered. Much work has since been done that is, as it were, tangential in interest to the kinked demand curve hypothesis, examples being the rather general works cited by Scherer (1970, 19) in support of the hypothesis. Rather less work has been done that attempts to examine the hypothesis in a direct way. The concern of this chapter will be with those empirical studies, following on from the earliest work, that have been specifically directed at the kinked demand curve hypothesis.

The seminal work of Stigler (1947), which is brilliant both as a theoretical and as an empirical study, will be taken as the starting point. Very often this work has been misunderstood. On the one hand, it is often quoted with approval, along with Hall and Hitch and Sweezy, as if this were to strengthen the plausibility of the kinked demand curve concept. In reality, Stigler's study tends to cast serious doubts on its plausibility. On the other hand, Stigler's study is often quoted as though it were definitive, and the last word on the subject. In fact it has been subjected to penetrating criticisms by Efroymson (1955), an authority who is followed closely in the next two sections, and a number of other studies of the kinked demand curve that have been published in more recent years. In view of these confusions, Stigler's study is considered with some thoroughness in sections 5.2 and 5.3.

It will prove convenient to classify tests of the kinked demand curve as involving *objective* and *subjective* evidence. The objective evidence consists of observable market phenomena, like list prices and the level of output; and the subjective evidence consists of opinions solicited from business men about what they believe their market environment to be. Broadly speaking the studies employing objective evidence stem from Stigler (1947) and the studies employing subjective evidence stem from Hall and Hitch (1939) and Sweezy (1939). Each of these approaches will be examined in turn in sections 5.4 and 5.5.

5.2.　　　Empirical Aspects of Stigler's Study:
Examining the Assumptions

Stigler distinguishes between two different methods of testing the kinked demand curve theory: the one involving tests of its assumptions, and the other involving tests of its implications, or predictions. This section will be concerned with the former method. Although the testing of assumptions is not regarded as a satisfactory procedure by all methodologists of economics, it may be of value if several rival explanations of price rigidity generate similar predictions.

According to Stigler, a firm (using this anonymous term to stand for an entrepreneur, a manager, a board of directors, etc. – whichever is appropriate) will have reason to believe in the kink if its price increases go unmatched by rivals and if its price cuts are followed by rivals. Thus it is his view that a proper empirical investigation should determine whether the price history of an industry might foster a belief on the part of a firm in the existence of a kinked demand curve. He does not investigate what firms actually claim to believe, the line followed by Hall and Hitch, but rather considers what market factors ought to lead firms to believe. In this way Stigler claims that it is possible to 'objectify' the basis for a kink.

This line of reasoning is contested by Efroymson (1955), who argues that only if a firm did not believe in the kink would it attempt a unilateral price increase. According to this view, objective evidence of the kink would only emerge when a firm had made a mistaken judgment. It should not be expected that a firm would stubbornly raise prices in the belief that it would not be followed, nor that it would lower prices believing it *would* be followed, for to such a firm these actions would be believed to reduce profits. It is for precisely this reason that the prevailing price constitutes a barrier to price revisions. This also makes clear the difficulty of testing for the kink by what we have called 'objective' means, the problem being that a firm which did believe in the kink would not vary its price.

Stigler's evidence for belief in the kinked demand curve is based on a study of the history of price movements in seven industries: cigarettes, automobiles, anthracite, steel, dynamite, gasoline and potash. Several of these histories are worth re-examining with the intention of comparing the interpretations put on them by Stigler and Efroymson. Consider, for example, the history of prices in the American cigarette industry from 1918 to 1934. The industry had three large firms, Reynolds (Camel), American Tobacco (Lucky Strike), and Liggett and Myers. Stigler's history starts with the unilateral price increase by American Tobacco: Lucky Strikes were raised in price from $6.00 to $7.50 per thousand, but rivals maintained their old prices. The sales of Lucky Strikes fell by almost a third in one month, and American Tobacco were forced to revoke the price increase. On the Stigler interpretation such an experience would create a belief in the kink. The Efroymson interpretation would agree with this, but would insert the caveat that prior to the event American Tobacco had obviously not believed in the kink. The two interpretations of the subsequent price history differ markedly. Subsequently to American Tobacco's unsuccessful pricing strategy, increases and reductions in prices were followed after a very short period, irrespective of which firm initiated the price change. According to Stigler (1947, 421) this evidence is 'not such as to create a belief in the existence of a kink'. According to Efroymson (1955, 125), 'the impressive evidence of the earlier period had not been forgotten', the implication being that firms, having been convinced of the kink, subsequently took steps to circumvent it by overt or covert collusion. As another example, consider Stigler's evidence on the u.s. steel industry. Two firms, United States Steel and Bethlehem, dominated the industry, and concealed price reductions on the list prices were widespread. Stigler reaches the conclusion that there is therefore no evidence of a kink, whereas Efroymson argues that belief in the kink by firms would encourage them to undertake covert price reductions of the kind observed in the steel industry.

Alternative explanations offered by Efroymson can be summarised easily by a diagram first introduced in chapter 4. In figure 5.1, the kinked demand curve is shown as being made up of segments of Chamberlin's dd' and DD' curves. The curve dAD' is the obtuse kinked demand curve and DAd' is the reflex kinked demand curve. According to Efroymson's interpretation, American Tobacco believed DA to be the relevant demand relationship for price increases, but found to its cost that it was actually dA. In the case of the steel industry, firms, believing in the existence of the obtuse kink dAD', attempted to avoid operating on the segment AD' by secret undercutting.

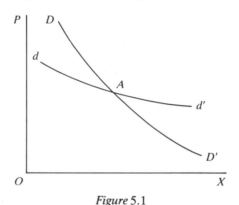

Figure 5.1

Finally, a point not given very serious consideration by Stigler in this part of his empirical work is that the demand curve may be shifting over time. The demand curve is an *ex ante* concept, and any single observation is but a point on the demand curve at a moment in time. Thus it may not be evident from the data whether a shift in price over time implies a movement along one or other segment of a stationary kinked demand curve, or whether it implies that the demand curve as a whole has shifted over time, thereby altering the position at which the kink occurs. If the latter is happening, the data on price changes would clearly reveal nothing about the form, or even the existence, of a kink.

To summarise: both Stigler and Efroymson are in agreement that objective price data can throw light on the existence or otherwise of a kink. Their point of departure is that Efroymson believes that such observations will be in the minority, arising only when a firm has made a misjudgment, whereas Stigler holds the view that the data may continually confirm or disconfirm belief in the kink. Obviously Efroymson's account of how firms behave is more plausible than Stigler's, as it takes account of adaption and learning. However, to say that firms that believe in the kink will then take steps to circumvent it, is tantamount to saying that firms, by modifying their behaviour, are also modifying their beliefs. If a firm has taken what steps it deems necessary to iron out the kink, does it make sense to say that the firm still believes in the kink? Thus Efroymson's analysis, though a helpful explanation of the behaviour of firms, may not have much operational significance.

5.3. Empirical Aspects of Stigler's Study: Examining the Implications

In the previous section Stigler's attempt to test the kinked demand curve hypothesis by testing its behavioural assumptions was examined. Some methodologists of economics would view this approach with suspicion, and would give greater emphasis to the predictive ability of a theory. This is what Stigler does in the second part of his famous study, and it is to the implications of the theory that this section is addressed.

Stigler's basic procedure is to compare the flexibility of prices in a collection of oligopolistic and non-oligopolistic American industries for a complete business cycle from June 1929 to May 1937. The basic test of price flexibility is the frequency of change of the monthly list price quotations, although the coefficient of variation (i.e. the standard deviation divided by the mean) is also reported. The flexibility tests are applied to four different market situations, most of which use the same basic data (reproduced, for reference purposes, in table 5.1). The first market situation compares nineteen oligopolies with two monopolies. Even though the monopolies experienced, on the whole, greater output variation than the oligopolies, they tended to have less flexible prices, measured both by price changes and by the coefficient of variation (see table 5.1).[1] According to Stigler's reason-

1. This tendency for quantity flexibility to replace price flexibility is quite familiar to contemporary economic theorists, but

Table 5.1
Measures of market structure for twenty-one products
and of their price flexibility and output variability
June 1929–May 1937. Extracted from Stigler (1947).

Product	No. of firms in industry	Price leader	No. of price changes	Coeff. of variation	Coeff. of variation of output
Oligopolies					
Bananas	2	yes	46	16	17
Boric acid	3	no	7	17	16
Cans	4	yes	6	5	27
Cement	12	no	14	11	41
Copper	4	no	63	37	43
Gasoline*	11	no	84	22	16
Grain-binder	2	yes	5	3	63
Linoleum	2	no?	12	9	30
Newsprint	9	no	6	16	16
Plaster	3	yes	4	5	29
Plate glass	2	no	8	13	34
Plows	6	no	25	6	50
Rayon	8	no	26	30	34
Soap	3	no	9	12	7
Starch	4	yes	20	12	13
Sulfur	2	yes	0	0	24
Tires	8	no	36	9	16
Tractors	4	yes	6	6	76
Window glass	3	no	20	21	24
Monopolies					
Aluminum	1		2	6	47
Nickel	1		0	0	35

*In Pennsylvania and Delaware

ing, this refutes the kinked demand curve theory, as a monopolist should completely 'iron-out' the kink, and thus remove any basis for price rigidity. The second situation compares the same five oligopolies (rayon, copper, pineapple canning, typewriters, midwestern oil) during, and outside of, periods of collusion. Prices tended to be significantly less flexible during collusion, again

in Stigler's time had only been given *ad hoc* treatment by economists like Means.

tending to refute the kinked demand curve theory, by a similar argument to that given in the previous case. The third situation compares oligopolies subject to 'dominant firm' price leadership with other oligopolies. It is argued that dominant firms would not have kinked demand curves, and hence that industries with price leaders should have more flexible prices than other types of oligopolistic industries. As a consultation of table 5.1 confirms, prices were *less* flexible in industries with price leaders than with other industries, refuting the kinked demand curve theory. The fourth situation compares six oligopolies producing heterogeneous goods (soap, tractors, grain-binders, plows, tires, linoleum) with thirteen oligopolies producing homogeneous goods (the remaining industries listed under oligopolies in table 5.1). The general tendency was for prices to be more flexible for industries producing homogeneous goods. This refutes the kinked demand curve hypothesis,[1] as greater homogeneity of the product would tend to make the kink more pronounced. This would increase the discontinuity in the marginal revenue curve, thus reinforcing the tendency to price rigidity. Another, but less satisfactory, test compares the price flexibilities of industries with different numbers of firms. By the kink theory, according to Stigler, the fewer the number of rivals, the greater the flexibility of prices, with the caveat that prices are likely to be least flexible with 'an intermediate number of rivals' (which he puts at five to ten firms). That is, the relationship between number of rivals and flexibility should be u-shaped. The evidence on this is not clear-cut, and indeed Efroymson dismisses the whole argument as 'obscure'. From table 5.1 it is evident that there is a weak tendency for an increase in the number of rivals to be associated with an increase in price flexibility, casting doubt on the hypothesis of a u-shaped relationship. However, as the precise number of firms was in doubt for more than half the industries listed, the validity of this test is highly dubious, and it will not be given further discussion.

Efroymson (1955) takes issue with Stigler's methods and conclusions on four counts. First, he disputes that Stigler's conclu-

1. It is, however, consistent with a number of other plausible explanations. For example, quality variation might be used as a substitute for price variation for heterogeneous goods. Further, for such goods a fixed price might be part of the marketing strategy (*cf.* the sixpenny bar of chocolate).

sions can be drawn from the time period used. Secondly, he points to pitfalls in the use of nominal rather than transaction prices. Thirdly, he contests the assumptions made about the kink under price leadership and collusion. Fourthly, he disagrees with the interpretation Stigler puts on the apparent relative price rigidities manifest in oligopolies producing heterogeneous, rather than homogeneous, goods.

Concerning the time period used, Efroymson's basic criticism is that, because it extended for a full business cycle, it embraced sub-periods in which firms might have behaved in different ways. As indicated in chapter 4, a basic tenet of Efroymson's position is that the form of the kink will be dependent on the buoyancy of the market, and indeed this view is endorsed by the original analysis of Sweezy (1939, 407–8). In depressed market conditions, the kink will be obtuse and of the form dAD' in figure 5.1, whereas in a buoyant or exuberant market when firms are working close to full capacity, the kink will be reflex, and of the form DAd'. In the latter case, prices will tend to be unstable. Another criticism that Efroymson levels at the use of the time period is that it does not distinguish between periods of abnormal business conditions in which price wars occur, and periods of more settled business conditions. Both price wars and the existence of a reflex kink would tend to raise any measure of price flexibility in oligopolies.

The use of transaction prices rather than list prices is obviously to be preferred in any test of the kinked demand curve hypothesis, and indeed Stigler is aware of this. However, he did, perforce, use list prices, and these will tend to understate the flexibility of prices. This would not present an insuperable problem were it true that the extent of the understatement of price flexibility were uniform between market structures. Unfortunately, this is not likely to be so, and Efroymson argues that it is particularly those oligopolies that practice collusion or price leadership that will practice off-list selling. Stigler cites the behaviour of a combination of rayon producers over the period 21 October 1931 to 23 May 1932. During this time there were no changes in list prices, from which Stigler concludes that the kink theory must be refuted, as collusion should lead to greater price variability. In reality, as a study by Markham (1952, 77) testifies, off-list selling was common: 'although no changes were made in the list price of rayon between October 21, 1931 and May 23, 1932, "misbranding" and off-list selling continued and by April . . . even such large producers as Viscose, Dupont and Industrial were selling rayon at 30 per cent below list price'. It is therefore necessary to be cautious in concluding that a reduction in *list price flexibility* as a result of collusion reflects a reduction in *transaction price flexibility*. Rather it may be that there is a greater correspondence between list and transaction prices before collusion than after collusion.

Following on from this point, Efroymson argues that there can be no presumption that collusion or the acceptance of price leadership will necessarily be successful in removing the kink, even if this is the intention of such actions. There will always be a fear that parties to a collusive arrangement will not conform, in which case the demand curve will tend to be obtusely kinked. The rayon producers' and the pineapple canners' and growers' agreements that Stigler cites refer to a period (1931–32) in which markets were depressed and there was a downward pressure on prices. Two major purposes of collusion in such situations are, first, to prevent a price war, and secondly, to buttress-up the price structure. In such a situation, one would expect a comparative stability of prices, rather than price flexibility, as implied by Stigler.

Finally, many of the factors other than the obtuse kink that Stigler mentions as promoting price stability ('costs of price changes', 'fear of government attention', etc.) apply equally to monopolies and oligopolies, and equally to oligopolies producing homogeneous or heterogeneous goods.[1] To Stigler the kinked demand curve must give *the* explanation of price rigidity in oligopolies *vis-à-vis* other market structures – or else be regarded as unimportant. Perhaps the obtuse kink does not give the sole, or even the major explanation, of price rigidity, but this does not mean that it is false as an explanation, nor that it should be dismissed as unimportant. It does of course imply that other

1. An obvious but important criticism neglected by Efroymson is that Stigler fails to establish that variation in determining factors (broadly speaking, tastes and technology) were similar between the two groups compared (*viz.* oligopolies and monopolies).

explanations for price rigidity in non-oligopolistic markets should be sought.

5.4.   *Further Objective Evidence*

Stigler (1947) established the lines of investigation that a number of economists were to pursue. The studies of Julian Simon (1969), Primeaux and Bomball (1974) and Primeaux and Smith (1976) are all of the same genus as the Stigler study, but in a number of respects attempt to make improvements on the original methodology. Even so, these later studies are themselves not without shortcomings, and some of their weaknesses will be examined. The studies of Cowling and Cubbin (1970) and Peel (1972) are new departures in terms of the use of 'objective' evidence, and are perhaps suggestive of the lines that future research might follow.

Simon (1969) attempts to improve on Stigler's methods in two respects. First, many more monopolies are considered rather than the meagre two in Stigler's original study. Secondly, the list prices chosen for analysis very often do not deviate, it is claimed, from the transaction prices. The 'good' analysed by Simon is advertising space in business magazines. The basic unit for which rates are quoted is a single insertion of a full-page black-and-white advertisement. Magazines are grouped according to classifications established by the Standard Rate and Data Service (SRDS), and each group contains from one to twenty-nine publications. Simon uses as basic data the year-end rates for each magazine for the two sub-periods 1955–61 and 1961–64. His measure of price flexibility is the number of changes in year-end rates (dubbed 'change years'), averaged over the number of magazines. This procedure can be made clear by the following example. Suppose there are two competitors, Magazine X and Magazine Y in a particular SRDS classification group called Z. Let their year-end rates (in dollars) be as follows:

	X	Y
1961	500	460
1962	510	460
1963	520	460
1964	520	470

For Magazine X there are two change years (1961–62 and 1962–63) and for Magazine Y there is one change year (1963–64). By the Simon method, the 'mean number of change years' is $(2 + 1)/2 = 1.5$. This statistic is computed for every other classification group that has two members, and then averaged over the classification groups to give the 'grand mean number of change years' for the two-member group size. This procedure is repeated for each group size. On the basis of this evidence it is concluded that prices do not change more frequently for groups with only one magazine compared to groups with two or more magazines. The inference drawn from this is that the kinked demand curve hypothesis has been falsified, presumably because the test is regarded as analogous to Stigler's test that compares the flexibility of monopoly prices with oligopoly prices.

However, the Simon case is clearly different in several respects. An obvious difference is that Simon is not comparing the prices set by various *firms*, but the prices set by various *magazines*. It is probable that for any group, several magazines are produced by the same firm, and less probable, though still likely, that some firms produce magazines that lie in several groups. This will have two implications. Firstly, for any group size, the number of effective competitors is overstated. Secondly, if a firm sells magazines in several groups and adopts a fairly uniform pricing strategy for its magazines, the likely effect is to reduce the between-group variability of prices. But even granted that a magazine can be treated as a firm, Simon's method is suspect. Stigler compares monopolies with oligopolies, whereas Simon compares monopolies with *any other market structure*. If, for most examples of an n-size group, the members were in collusion, then by the Stigler reasoning there would be no kink and prices should be as flexible as under monopoly. No attempt is made by Simon to distinguish the non-collusive oligopolies (the proper objects of the test, according to Stigler's methodology) from collusive oligopolies, price leadership, competitive markets, etc.

As Machlup (1952, 463) has emphasised, it is important to know what is meant by the price of a good. On the obvious level, there may be problems of adjusting for rebates, taxes, commissions, etc., but more seriously, there may be problems of adjusting for the quality and specification of the good. The rate per page that Simon considers in computing the number of change years is not the effective price. As Simon himself points out, the effective price is the rate per page divided by the number of readers. As a footnote example given by Simon (1969, 973) indicates, the effective price will be different for almost every year, given year-to-year variations in circulation. That is, were the change year calculations to be repeated using effective prices rather than the rate per page, the mean number of change years would be almost identical for all group sizes. For example, for the 1961–64 sub-period, it would be near three in all cases, and clearly such data could throw no light on questions of relative price flexibility. Simon suggests that, if anything, the smaller the group size, the greater the circulation changes, though he only investigates circulation figures for the one- and two-magazine groups. This would tend to confirm his claim, though a new measure of flexibility would have to be used, the coefficient of variation used by Stigler being the most obvious choice.

On purely statistical grounds, a number of further criticisms can be made of Simon's procedure. For both the sub-periods considered, the dispersion of change years was very slight. For example, for the sub-period 1955–61, the number of change years was approximately 2.4, on average, with the range being from 1.81 to 2.95. It would be difficult for any statistical test to discriminate between such small variations as those exhibited by Simon's data. For group sizes with few members the consequences of measurement error could be serious with data already lacking richness of variation. Simon claims that within-year price changes are rare, but to the extent that they exist at all, they could make an appreciable difference to the computed average number of changes. In particular, and contrary to Simon's assertion, the number of changes for the most flexible prices will be biased downwards. Put another way, there will be a tendency for the more flexible prices to look as rigid as the genuinely rigid prices. Finally, Simon's procedure of computing 'grand means' is likely to smooth out a lot of the natural variability present in the data: indeed this is generally the purpose of computing a mean. Suppose, to extend the example used earlier, that Magazines X and Y and Magazines A and B are the only members of the two-magazine group size, and that Magazine A has three change years, as has Magazine *B*. The mean number of change years for Magazines *A* and *B* is $(3+3)/2 = 3.0$. The corresponding figure for Magazines *X* and *Y* has already been computed as 1.5, and hence Simon's 'grand mean number of change years' is $(1.5+3.0)/2 = 2.25$. What the averaging process does is to conceal the greater variability of prices for Magazines *A* and *B*: information that is highly relevant to any test of the kinked demand curve hypothesis. Therefore, on statistical grounds, the Simon study is probably best regarded as inconclusive.

An important study, which builds on the works of Stigler and Simon but avoids several of the pitfalls of these works, is the investigation by Primeaux and Bomball (1974) using data on municipally owned and privately owned electric utilities in the United States. The strong features of the study are as follows. First, the good in question is well defined. Each category of kilowatt-hours is treated as a distinct product and the price is taken from the appropriate rate schedule. There is no problem of adjusting to get the effective price, nor any problem of a divergence between list price and transaction price, as discounts on the published price schedules are illegal for public utilities. Secondly, the influence of the type of product on the recorded number of price changes is removed. In the Stigler study, comparisons of price flexibility are made for firms producing quite different goods. It was shown in chapter 2 that the length of the discontinuity in the marginal revenue curve, which is the cause of price inflexibility, is dependent on the difference between the elasticities of the two segments of the kinked demand curve. This in turn depends on the homogeneity of the good, the discontinuity tending to be greater, the more homogeneous the good. Thus differences in price flexibility might be due to differences in the degree of kinkiness of the demand curves, rather than to differences in market structure. The Primeaux and Bomball study compares monopolies supplying electricity with duopolies supplying electricity, thus holding constant any influence that the degree of substitution may have on price flexibility. Thirdly, in this study the comparison between market structures is balanced, and furthermore, the types of market structure are known very precisely. The study compares seventeen cities having duopolistic competition (one private, one municipal firm) with twenty-two municipal monopolies. Thus there is no imbalance in the representation of oligopolies *vis-à-vis* monopolies, as in Stigler's study. As important, the chosen duopolies come from cities in which a municipally owned firm and a privately owned firm are in direct competition, in the sense that a customer can switch at will from one electricity supplier to the other. This is in contrast to Simon's study, in which it is not clear whether the 'firms' in the two-firm group are competing or colluding.

However, the methods of analysis used by Primeaux and Bomball (1974) still retain some of the shortcomings of Stigler (1947) and Simon (1969). Two basic tests are used. First, the numbers of price changes for the duopoly and monopoly subsets are compared. Annual price data for the period 1959–70 are used, with 1963 excluded, for reasons of re-classification. As in Simon's study, the difficulty arises that some firms change prices more than once a year, though the authors claim this rarely happens. Another difficulty created by annual data is that the sequence in which price changes take place may be masked. This is relevant to the second test used by Primeaux and Bomball, which examines whether rivals follow price increases and decreases. They report 48 simultaneous price changes for the 1959–70 period as compared to 84 changes that were not followed within three years. It is possible that the use of annual data has overstated the number of simultaneous price increases.

The grand mean of change years is computed by an identical procedure to that used by Simon (1969), though it cannot be subject to such strong criticism in this case, as firms are selling a homogeneous good, and only two group sizes are involved, each containing rather similar numbers of firms. Table 5.2, which is reproduced from Primeaux and Bomball (1974, 857), clearly indicates that, product for product, prices were more flexible in the duopolistic markets than in the monopolies. The authors' contention is that this refutes the kinked demand curve hypothesis. Unfortunately, the hypothesis has not been modified by the argument of Efroymson (1943, 1955) to the effect that the kink may be obtuse or reflex, depending on whether the industry is below, or close to, full capacity. In the former case, price rigidity is implied; in the latter case, price flexibility. Primeaux and Bomball (1974, 854) state that they are not concerned with

Table 5.2
Number of price changes.
Extracted from Primeaux and Bomball (1974, 857)

1959–62				1964–70		
kWh	No. of price changes	Grand Mean No. of change years		kWh	No. of price changes	Grand Mean No. of change years
			Monopoly			
25	1	0.05		100	14	0.64
40	2	0.09		250	19	0.86
100	4	0.18		500	22	1.00
250	4	0.18		750	23	1.05
500	5	0.23		1000	24	1.09
			Duopoly			
25	9	0.27		100	35	1.03
40	9	0.27		250	42	1.24
100	9	0.27		500	42	1.24
250	10	0.29		750	48	1.41
500	11	0.32		1000	52	1.53

Source: data extracted from FPC's *Typical Electric Bills*, various years

the sort of economic conditions that, on the Efroymson argument, would be associated with the obtuse kink: 'The data do not include years of depressed economic conditions which could abnormally reflect on pricing behaviour'. Thus there is some suspicion that the results might equally be interpreted as providing support for the *reflex* kinked demand curve. This suspicion is strengthened by a further consideration of the second test, which is based on the data given in table 5.3. In general, the municipally controlled firms were not subject to regulatory price constraints, whereas the privately owned firms were. If allowance is made for the consequent time lag in price adjustments by privately owned firms, the general pattern that emerges is that price increases are more nearly simultaneous than are price decreases. This apparently refutes the unrevised version of the kinked demand curve theory, but is consistent with the modified version of Efroymson, in which the reflex kink prevails in good economic conditions.

The most recent attempt (as of the time of writing) to test the

Table 5.3
Price increases and decreases.
Extracted from Primeaux and Bomball (1974, 858)

1.	Price increases not followed (within 3 years)	42
2.	Price decreases not followed (within 3 years)	42
3.	Simultaneous price changes	48
	Increases	20
	Opposite	10
	Decreases	18
4.	Delay in following price increases	18
	1 year	18
5.	Delay in following price decreases	15
	1 year	10
	2 years	5
6.	Delay in changing in the opposite direction	11
	Municipal initiated a decrease, 1-year delay in increasing	2
	Private initiated a decrease, 1-year delay in increasing	4
	Private initiated a decrease, 3-year delay in increasing	5

Source: data extracted from FPC's *Typical Electric Bills*, various years

kinked demand curve hypothesis along Stigler lines is the study made by Primeaux and Smith (1976) of the U.S. pharmaceutical industry. In some ways the study represents a step back from the advance made in Primeaux and Bomball (1974) because a number of unfortunate features of the Simon (1969) study are reintroduced. In particular, the study looks at drug *products,* rather than at drug-producing *firms,* and this is subject to the kinds of criticism elaborated earlier in the context of Simon's study. The criteria involved in classifying drug products into monopoly, duopoly and oligopoly categories are complex. The authors provide little information on this matter, but claim they are confident in the classification adopted because one of the authors is a pharmacist. Certainly, the expert knowledge of a pharmacist is necessary for an evaluation of which chemically distinct products should nevertheless be regarded as closely related in terms of the ailments they are used to treat. Equally, however, expert economic judgment, plus rather full information, is required to make the final judgment on how a market should be classified. Obvious problems spring to mind immediately. For example, suppose a single firm produces two different drugs for treating a known ailment, and that in medical terms the effectiveness of each drug is broadly similar in terms of therapeutic benefits per dollar. Presumably a pharmacist would regard such drugs as rivalrous, but an economist would also want to know whether the firm, in selling these drugs, permitted sufficiently independent pricing in these lines to warrant their being placed in a duopoly category. Even if many *different* firms produce drugs that a pharmacist might regard as rivalrous, an economist should not immediately classify such a situation as oligopolistic competition until it is clear that collusive behaviour is absent. Unless such precautions are taken in establishing categories, Stigler-type tests have little meaning.

The annual price data on which the study is based were obtained from the *Drug Topics Red Book* for the years 1964 to 1970, suggesting that list prices, rather than the more desirable trans-action prices, were used. As in Simon (1969) and Primeaux and Bomball (1974), the use of annual data tends to bias downwards the observed price variation of the more flexibly priced products. Primeaux and Smith use the two basic Stigler tests (number of price changes, and concordance of price changes) and compute the numbers of change years as in the Simon study. A chi-square test applied to the grand means of number of changes was unable to detect statistically significant differences in variability between the monopolies, duopolies and oligopolies. This is perhaps not surprising in view of the criticisms made above of the similar data used by Simon, but without the application of significance tests. When lags in price changes are taken into account, the general pattern that emerges is a tendency for price increases to be followed and for price decreases to go unmatched. Such evidence is consistent with a reflex kinked demand curve, but is regarded by the authors as sufficient to refute the conventional kinked demand curve hypothesis. In fact evidence for the obtuse kink is far from absent, especially for the duopolies. This prompts the thought that an examination of capacity utilisation for the various categories studied might suggest the effects of capacity on the obtuseness or reflexivity of the demand curve, and thus might ultimately lead to a reconciliation of the data with a more general kinked demand curve theory.

Finally, two British studies by Cowling and Cubbin (1970) and

Peel (1972) do not follow the Stigler methodology, but may yet be regarded as throwing some light on the kinked demand curve hypothesis. Both studies are concerned with the British motor industry over the period 1955–68. Cowling and Cubbin make a distinction between the list price and a quality-adjusted, or hedonic, price. They suggest that the demand curve facing a manufacturer is kinked at the list price for an established model. This will be so, they reason, because rivals can retaliate by changing their own list prices in a relatively short period: a 'short' period being one in which cost and demand conditions do not alter substantially. However, if price is effectively varied by altering the quality of a car, typically by the introduction of a new model, retaliation cannot occur so rapidly, for two reasons. First, there may be doubts on the part of rivals whether an implicit price reduction has occurred, which may lead to a 'wait and see' policy being adopted until a shift in market share is observed. Secondly, a rival, unable to respond by quality variation in the short run, may be loath to respond by list price variation, for fear that such an overt act might precipitate a price war. For the period studied, new models were generally introduced at an annual Motor Show, meaning that appropriate retaliation by rivals in terms of quality variation could not occur for a year. This being the case, the demand curve for new models should be unkinked. Thus quality adjusted prices should be more flexible than list prices, because of the absence of a kink in the demand schedule for new models, and the existence of a kink in that for established models. This conjecture is confirmed by the evidence. The coefficient of variation for a price index of established models is 1.63, whereas it is 5.29 for a chain hedonic index constructed by methods explained in Cowling and Cubbin (1970). Thus their research suggests that the demand curve for established models was kinked at the list price. Peel (1972) pursues this analysis further, and argues that the demand curve for labour in this industry has a discontinuity, as for the product's marginal revenue curve, and that on an Efroymson (1943) type of argument, this discontinuity should be smaller, the closer the firm is to capacity. This leads to the conclusion that below full capacity unions will push hard for wage rate increases, that this pushfulness will diminish as capacity increases (and therefore as the discontinuity in the labour demand curve diminishes), and that this pushfulness will rise again as full capacity is reached. This leads Peel to postulate a U-shaped relationship between militancy (as measured by percentage change in hourly earnings, $\dot{w}$) and excess demand (as measured by percentage changes in the registration of new models, D). A regression of $\dot{w}$ on D which is quadratic in D, using data for 1955–68, produced highly significant coefficients, the expected positive coefficient for the quadratic term, and an adjusted R^2 of 0.31. Thus, for the British motor industry at least, there seems to be evidence for a kinked demand curve in both the product and factor markets.

5.5. *The Subjective Evidence*

In this chapter a distinction has been drawn between the 'objective' and 'subjective' evidence on the kinked demand curve. The previous section has been concerned exclusively with the so-called objective evidence. The approach to be examined in this section tries to understand the economic world by a different method. It involves examining the subjective evidence supplied to the economist by the business man. The starting point for obtaining such evidence is the construction of a questionnaire, this being a standardised set of questions that can be distributed quite impersonally to a sample of firms. A development of this procedure is the interview method. In this method the questionnaire is completed whilst an investigator is present. The investigator usually can help to clarify the questionnaire in several respects, and may be at liberty to pose more open-minded questions, but in general his initiative is somewhat limited. Finally, there is the case-study approach, in which the investigator attempts to become totally immersed in those activities of the firm that are being examined.

The path from a questionnaire to an interview to a case study involves the introduction of an increasing degree of subjectivity into the process of investigation. This has obvious disadvantages from the viewpoint of scientific method. The more subjective the investigation, the greater is the danger that the interaction between the investigator and his subject will produce biased results. Furthermore, the more subjective the investigation, the less likely it is to meet the scientific criterion of replicability. If Joe

Bain can obtain remarkably illuminating information by performing a case study of a firm, is this to be regarded as a *scientific* achievement if nobody but Joe Bain could have gathered such information? On the other hand, the more subjective the investigation, the greater is its potential for culling fruitful material – though whether this potential will necessarily be achieved is another matter. It will not be assumed in this section that there is a *prima facie* case for any one technique of investigation over another; but merely that there are more or less adequate ways of applying any technique.

Subjectivity clearly is involved in the investigation procedures described above. But more than this, the object of inquiry itself, namely the opinion of a business man, is also subjective in character. It is in this latter sense that the evidence to be reported in this section is to be regarded as 'subjective'. No matter how subjectively formulated, opinions are a worthwhile object of inquiry if business men act on their opinions.

It has been shown in chapter 2 that early attempts at discovering the opinions of business men were relatively unsophisticated. A similar criticism can be levelled at the somewhat later study of Shackle (1955), although the work of Barback (1964), which builds directly on that of Shackle, is a significant advance in the gathering of subjective evidence. Shackle (1955) presented a questionnaire to a society of businessmen engaged in engineering production on Merseyside. Barback (1964) used a modified version of this questionnaire as the basis for a detailed case-study investigation of seven rather small British firms, most of which were engaged in clothing manufacturing. On a much larger scale is the classical enquiry of Fog (1960) into the pricing policies of 139 Danish manufacturers over the period 1951 to 1955. This enquiry was largely carried out by the interview method. More recently a major contribution has been made to the literature of industrial economics by the publications of Nowotny and Walther (1978a, b) on the pricing policies of Austrian enterprises. The basic technique of investigation was the questionnaire, but this was supplemented by personal interviews. Of course, many other studies of pricing policy have been conducted, but surprisingly few provide illumination on the kinked demand curve, possibly because one only obtains the necessary useful information for such a specific hypothesis by conscious volition. In keeping with the spirit of the earlier part of this chapter, the purpose of this section is to look at only those studies that have been directly concerned with obtaining subjective evidence on the kinked demand curve.

The phrase 'systematic impressionism' is used by Shackle (1955, 40) to describe his attempt to test the claim that entrepreneurs try to maximise net revenue. He was invited to give an after-dinner address to a society of businessmen engaged in engineering production and commerce on Merseyside, and decided to use his guests to provide 'clinical evidence' on behaviour within the firm. A questionnaire was to provide the basis for this evidence, and Shackle reports that he devoted about 50 minutes to explaining the questions and to relating the answer options to economic theory. He then asked each guest to allot a mark of between zero and ten to each of the answer options. From the reported results, it seems that seventeen guests were present. The businessmen were in effect asked to give opinions on three questions: what does the businessman seek to maximise; how does the businessman decide his price; and how does the businessman reach his investment decisions. The second question was posed through the phrase: 'The businessman decides the price of his product in the following way.' The possible ways were marginal cost pricing, full cost pricing, etc., and included the option that 'I have to reckon that a lowering of my price will be followed by a lowering of my rivals' prices, but a raising of my price will not be imitated by them'. This latter description of pricing is the kinked demand curve hypothesis in its unadorned 'obtuse kink' form. It got rather limited support: 61 marks out of a possible 170, as compared to, for example, 65/170 for marginalism and 75/170 for full cost pricing. However, immediate objections can be raised. The question does not make clear whether the businessman in general, or the respondent himself, is being referred to. Moreover, the kinked demand curve hypothesis is not really a hypothesis about price-setting, as is the full-cost hypothesis for example, but is a hypothesis about the conjectures of businessmen. Barback (1964) later used a modified version of Shackle's questionnaire, which specifically referred to 'your price-policy' rather than to that of 'the businessman' in general or in particular. The kinked demand curve answer option remained the same in essentials, the only changes being that 'I' and 'my' were altered to 'we' and 'our'. The seven firms of the sample should not be regarded as representative of any particular industrial situation. The initial approaches to firms were based on personal contacts and private introductions. All of the firms investigated were small to medium sized, with work forces ranging from a few people to several hundred. The enquiry was conducted as follows. First, the businessman was handed a modified version of the Shackle questionnaire. The answer options were discussed with him, and explanations were given where they were necessary. Marks were then allotted to the various answer options in an unhurried environment. Finally, a long discussion followed in which the businessman explained the way he had allotted his marks. On the basis of the summary results given by Barback (1964, 62) it seems that the most favoured price policy was that described by a kinked demand curve strategy (48 points out of a possible 70 points). The next most favoured policy was that of a flexible mark-up. A number of interesting points emerged as a result of the discussions that followed each allotting of marks. For example, a businessman from a lace finishing firm accepted the kinked demand curve statement, but qualified it by saying that when supply was very short the firm became faced with a seller's market and price might be quoted without regard for rivals. A spokesman for a raincoat manufacturing firm gave the kinked demand curve fair support, especially if lags in adjustment were allowed for. He, too, mentioned that the firm would take advantage of a seller's market, usually by the device of slightly differentiating an existing product, and then adding an extra margin on to its normal price. Statements such as these lend credence to the view of Efroymson (1943) that in buoyant markets, when firms are producing close to full capacity, businessmen may be optimistic about the consequences of a price increase.

By contrast to Barback's study, Fog's study of Danish manufacturing uses a much larger sample. The richness of information for any one firm is somewhat less, as the interview method rather than the case study method was used to gather the subjective evidence. Fog's sample is made up of two sub-samples: the 'material proper', consisting of rather full information on the pricing policies of 139 firms; and the 'supplementary material', consisting of incomplete information on an additional 47 firms. The material was collected over the period 1951 to 1955, and the main criterion for including a manufacturing firm was that it could provide usable information. A significant improvement on Barback's sample is that large firms are well represented. On the other hand, small and inefficient firms are probably under-represented. As in the Barback analysis, a questionnaire was used as the working basis for the study, but it is evident that much of the information gathered goes beyond what could have been obtained by a strict questionnaire format. The question that is relevant to the kinked demand curve hypothesis refers to the firm's anticipated sales:

How much more or less do you think you would be able to sell per month if the price were:

(a) reduced by 10 per cent?
(b) reduced by 20 per cent?
(c) increased by 10 per cent?
(d) increased by 20 per cent?

(Fog 1960, 10)

The form of this question can be criticised on several grounds. It is not clear whether account is to be taken of the reactions of competitors, or whether their prices should be taken as given. The question is not formulated in a way that permits the interviewee to qualify his response by indicating whether business conditions might influence his estimates. In reality, Fog reports, what the interviewee tended to do was first to make appropriate amendments to the question, and then to supply answers. The overall impression that Fog (1960, 130) obtained was that: 'Firms generally expect any reduction in price will be followed quickly by a corresponding reduction in the prices of competitors. On the other hand, there is greater uncertainty as to whether competitors will follow suit in case of a price increase'. This, of course, is the conventional obtuse kinked demand curve case which is being described. Unfortunately, there is no way of checking from Fog's study how widespread the phenomenon was, because no summary table of the answers to the questionnaire is provided. Several variants of the kinked demand curve are reported. For example, the doubly kinked demand curve of Gutenberg (1955,

1965) is described as capturing the comments of a number of interviewees. To take an example, Fog (1960, 43) reports that the spokesman for a shoe polish company said: 'There is a definite price interval. If the price rises above this interval, sales decrease. If the price drops below the interval, sales increase – but there is a growing risk that manufacturers of other brands of shoe polish will be forced to follow suit'. Another variant described by Fog (1960, 142) is the reversed kink demand curve, which he uses to explain the behaviour of small firms dominated by one or more large firms.

Similar in scale to the Fog study, but more impressive in the coherence of evidence is the work of Nowotny and Walther (1978a, b), the first citation being an article-length account of part of the material in the second citation. The basic technique of investigation was the questionnaire, but this was supplemented by personal interviews. The questionnaire was very detailed, and contained four sections of which the last ('Sales and Competition', containing sixteen questions) is most relevant to the kinked demand curve hypothesis. The sample was made up of Austrian firms with sales of over A.S. 100 m. A total of 509 questionnaires was sent out, of which 214 were returned in a usable form. The average response rate was 42 per cent, varying from 78 per cent in electronics to only 20 per cent in mining and leather manufacturing. Although the sample was large, it should not be regarded as strictly representative. In particular, the most over-represented industry was electronics, and the most under-represented was the clothing industry. The dominant market form in the sample was oligopoly. About 67 per cent of the firms were selling their main product in markets with at most nine other competitors.

The questionnaire design constitutes a significant advance over that of Fog (1960) and Barback (1964). Contrast for example the question used by Fog to elicit information on expected sales with the one used by Nowotny and Walther for the same purpose. The former question has been quoted above, the latter question runs as follows:

How would the sales of articles in the main product group react to a 5 % price change, supposing that competitors do not react, and that business conditions are normal:

(1) For a price cut of 5% the amount purchased would
   (a) increase more than 5%
   (b) increase less than 5%
   (c) increase by approximately 5%
   (d) not increase at all
   (e) not be possible to estimate
(2) For a price increase of 5% the amount purchased would
   (a) fall more than 5%
   (b) fall less than 5%
   (c) fall by approximately 5%
   (d) not fall at all
   (e) not be possible to estimate
(Nowotny and Walther 1978b, qu. 2, part IV of questionnaire)
The conditions surrounding the price change are made clear, and
the possibility of not knowing is also considered. A general
feature of the questionnaire is that it makes a distinction between
normal, boom and recession phases of the business cycle. Other
notable features are that it investigates market shares and degree
of product differentiation. The results most relevant to the
kinked demand curve hypothesis are summarised in table 5.4. It
is clear from this table that there is a general expectation in
normal and recession conditions that a price cut will be matched
and that a price increase will be reluctantly matched, if matched
at all. Expectations of this kind are more convergent in a reces-

Table 5.4
Expected reactions by competitors to price changes.
Extracted from Nowotny and Walther (1978, 55)

Expected rival reaction:		Price Reduction			Price Increase		
Rivals react with parallel price changes		1-10	Firm's market share (%) 11-50	>50	1-10	11-50	>50
In 'normal'	yes	61	81	65	46	51	59
business conditions	no	29	14	20	43	45	24
In boom periods	yes	32	37	31	68	74	71
	no	54	58	55	21	22	14
In recessions	yes	78	93	78	18	20	29
	no	7	4	8	68	75	57

sion than in normal times. This implies an obtuse kink, which becomes less kinked as business conditions improve. In boom conditions, the seller's market phenomenon observed by Fog emerges. Firms generally expect price reductions to be unmatched, and price increases to be followed. This implies that a reflex kink of the Efroymson (1943) type will pertain to boom periods. It is evident from table 5.4 that these results are most clear-cut for firms in the intermediate class, with market shares of between 11 and 50 per cent. It is in exactly such markets that one would most expect oligopolistic interdependence. Furthermore, this is the modal class of the study, containing 67 per cent of respondents. This impressionistic conclusion on the significance of the results is strengthened in the study by the application of a chi-square test. This test regards ideal confirmation of the kinked demand curve as implying a distribution of 100 per cent 'yes' answers for a price decrease and 100 per cent 'no' answers for a price increase. The alternative of no kink would imply an equal distribution of 'yes' and 'no' answers. For the intermediate group, the chi-square test reveals the kink as being highly significant.

The finding of Nowotny and Walther that the phase of the business cycle makes a difference to pricing in oligopoly is in keeping with the analysis of Efroymson (1943, 1955) and with the findings of Barback (1964) and Fog (1960). However, it is at variance with the finding of Cyert (1955), and with the implicit assumption of the study by Stigler (1947), that pricing in oligopolies is unaffected by the phase of the business cycle. In fact, the results of Cyert (1955) are not to be taken too seriously as they refer to only three oligopolies, the cigarette, automobile and potash industries. The null hypothesis is not rejected. In the case of the automobile industry, it was found that there was a significant difference in the pattern of price changes in different phases of the business cycle. The tests used, which are all non-parametric, are known to have rather low power, that is, roughly speaking, rather low ability to reject the null hypothesis. This being so, it is probably safer to reserve judgment than to accept the null hypothesis. More recent work by Stigler and Kindahl (1970) casts further doubt on Cyert's finding, and indeed, on the initial presumption of Stigler (1947). Stigler and Kindahl report on two reference cycle contractions (July 1957 to April 1958 and May 1960 to February 1961), and on two reference cycle expansions (April 1958 to May 1960 and November 1964 to November 1966). From this evidence it appears that price increases are more frequent in expansions, and price decreases are more frequent in contractions.

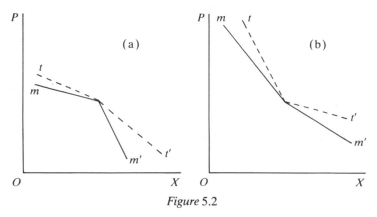

Figure 5.2

In section 5.3, Stigler's analysis of the consequences of heterogeneity for the kink was examined. Until the recent study of Nowotny and Walther (1978), no further serious consideration had been given to this matter. Nowotny and Walther show that in normal business conditions there is an asymmetry between the expected actions of rivals for price increases and price decreases, and that this asymmetry becomes more pronounced the more homogeneous is the product. Put more succinctly, the more homogeneous is the product, the more pronounced is the kink. This pattern is shown to be significant under a chi-square test. The same general pattern is observed in recession conditions, but alters in boom conditions. Paradoxically, in boom conditions the kink (or, more strictly, the reflex kink) becomes more pronounced the greater the degree of product differentiation. Nowotny and Walther (1978, 63) suggest that this may occur because a firm producing a highly differentiated product at, or near, full capacity output, might no longer consider price to be an important variable in the marketing strategy. These findings can be summarised by figure 5.2(a) and (b), which are corrected versions of the diagrams given in Nowotny and Walther (1978, 58). Diagram (a) refers to normal and recessionary conditions, whilst diagram (b) refers to boom conditions. In each diagram the kinked demand curve for a highly differentiated, or hetero-geneous, product is given by the dotted line tt', and the kinked demand curve for a slightly differentiated, or homogeneous, product is given by the solid line mm'.

Finally, this study also provides information on the doubly kinked demand curve of Gutenberg (1955, 1965). Question 6 of part IV of the questionnaire asked: 'Do you believe you have a certain amount of elbow room in pricing, within which a price change calls forth no reaction from competitors?' A supplementary question enquired into the extent of this elbow-room, or neutral price range. For 71 per cent of the sample, this elbow-room was put at less than 4 per cent. Furthermore, the more differentiated was the product, the more likely was a firm to report the existence of this neutral range.

5.6.   *Conclusion*

Two types of evidence on the kinked demand curve hypothesis have been identified, the 'objective' and the 'subjective'. In broad terms, the objective evidence has tended to refute the hypothesis and the subjective evidence to support it. However, both types of evidence must be handled carefully if they are not to do anything but cloud the issue. The intrinsic weakness of the Stigler approach is that it has no clearly specified standard of comparison. If prices are declared to be relatively rigid in an industry, the question arises: relatively rigid compared to what? If the standard of comparison is regarded as perfect competition, then it is of little consequence to compare the industries under examination with, for example, collusive oligopolies. As Mach-lup (1952, 474) has wittily observed, 'the adherents of the kink theory probably took it for granted that collusion resulted in price rigidity; they merely wished to show why prices could be rigid even under non-collusive oligopoly'. The intrinsic weakness of the subjective approach is its reliance on the questionnaire technique. The view of a number of microeconomists, most notably Machlup (1946) and Bain (1949), is that a questionnaire can never capture the very specific nature of a particular firm in terms of its technology, customs, management, etc. Answers are often mere rationalisations, and may even be dishonest rationalisations at that. To such critics, there is no substitute for the intensive case-study approach, slow and laborious though this may be. It is therefore apparent that, significant as is the contribution of Primeaux and Bomball (1974) to the objective evidence, and important as is the work of Nowotny and Walther (1978) for the subjective evidence, methods of testing the kinked demand curve hypothesis must still be refined and developed.

6

Conclusion

6.1. *The Current State of the Theory*

In chapters 2, 3 and 4 a fairly full development of the theoretical aspects of the kinked demand curve was provided. It was shown that the kinked demand curve may be regarded as a type of contingent demand curve. However, the informational requirements for constructing such demand curves are high. It seems inevitable therefore that the informational aspects of the kinked demand curve theory will receive the greatest attention in the future. A start in this direction has already been made.

For example, Cyert and de Groot (1971) analyse a duopoly model in which one of the firms is able to learn over time the maximum price up to which its rival will match a price increase. However, certain essential features of the kinked demand curve are missing: the good is homogeneous, implying an extreme version of the kinked demand curve with the upper segment infinitely elastic; and the analysis is more akin to price leadership (in that one firm is the aggressor and the other the responder) than conjectural oligopoly.

Stiglitz (1979), Scitovsky (1978) and Braverman (1980) emphasise the way in which informational asymmetries may lead to the kinked demand curve. Stiglitz considers the case of a market equilibrium in which new entrants are the only buyers searching for the lowest price, existing buyers being content with their purchases. If a firm in such a market were to raise its price, then marginal buyers, who were previously just satisfied, would join the ranks of newly entering buyers in searching for the lowest price, causing this firm to lose sales. On the other hand, should this firm lower its price, there would be no immediate gains in sales from customers of other firms who were in ignorance of this price cut. The only additional sales would be generated by the price-searching, newly entering, buyers. This interpretation of the kinked demand curve in dynamic terms is more satisfactory from a theoretical point of view than static versions of the kink, which tell rather strained stories of how adjustments take place *within* a suitably defined time period.

Scitovsky (1978) also argues that informational asymmetry can cause a kinked demand curve. If the price of a good is increased, then those customers who previously bought it might purchase less, or nothing at all. If price is cut, these customers might buy more, and, in addition, new customers will emerge who had previously not bought the good at all. New customers will only be attracted if they are at least to some extent exploratory in their purchases, or if the price-cutting firm advertises. There is thus an informational asymmetry between established and new customers, the former being almost immediately aware of a price cut because they make regular purchases of the good, and the latter being generally ignorant of a price cut, until a chance purchase, or advertising, alters this situation. For such cases, there will be an obtuse kinked demand curve. What Scitovsky describes as an 'addiction asymmetry' can cause a reflex kink. A price reduction accompanied by advertising can induce more people to buy a good, but if people are reluctant to abandon the habit of buying a good, a price increase might not induce them to buy markedly less. Such behaviour would generate a reflex kink, with the associated two possible equilibrium points, first mentioned in chapter 2. Scitovsky argues that informational and addictional asymmetries can lead to periodic sales drives with firms being willing to meet the informational costs of advertising, in order to move from a high-price, low-volume equilibrium position (on the upper branch of the reflex kink) to a low-price, high-volume position (on the lower branch). Once a larger market has become 'addicted' to the good, this short-term stratagem will tend to be abandoned, in favour of a more regular one that takes advantage of 'addiction' to the product. Braverman (1980) too advances an explanation for the reflex kink in terms of informational asymmetries, and does so in a framework that is explicitly probablistic. In his model consumers are identical and know the distribution of prices, but not the specific price in a specific shop. The cost of acquiring this latter information differs among consumers, and the distribution of these costs over customers is assumed to be known by shops. Each consumer is assumed to be a utility maximiser, and hence will choose to become informed of the lowest-price shop if the utility associated with the cost of information plus the price of the cheapest store is greater than the expected utility from purchasing randomly. All shops are assumed to have identical U-shaped cost curves, and to maximise profits under the assumption of zero conjectural variation. There are no barriers to entry. In such a model, Braverman shows that there is an asymmetry between a (small) price increase and a (small) price reduction. If one firm out of n increases its price, consumers will have a high probability of encountering one of the $(n-1)$ lower-priced firms by random choice. However, if one firm cuts its price, the consumer is unlikely to discover this unless he purchases information. Therefore the incentive to become informed of a unilateral price cut is $(n-1)$ times that of an equivalent unilateral price increase. Furthermore, considering only informed customers (assumed a fraction, k, of the population, m), it is clear that a unilateral price-increasing shop gets $(1-k)/m$ uninformed customers, which is k/m less than its equilibrium share of $1/m$. On the other hand, a unilateral price-cutting shop gets all informed customers plus its random share of uninformed customers, thus raising its share by $k(m-1)/m$ to a value of $k+(1-k)/m$. That is, the gain to a price cutter is $(m-1)$ times the loss to a price-raiser. Considered together, the two effects described above imply that a price cut gains $(m-1)^2$ as many customers as an equal price raise loses. In this way, a reversed kinked demand curve is produced.

Finally, Sengupta (1967), in an important but largely unrecognised analysis, has applied a transition probability model to the analysis of kinks in demand and cost curves, and specifically in the selling expenses function. Transition probabilities are defined for the probability that price is raised from p to $p+z$ or lowered from p to $p-y$, for z and y positive. An expected discounted profit function is set up, and using dynamic programming methods bounds are established for the optimal returns under both the price-increasing and price-decreasing policies. In this way, it is shown that keeping price unchanged can be optimal, providing an explanation of price rigidity that is a consequence of maximising long-run net profits. In a series of models, Sengupta (1967, ch. 8, 9) develops his analysis for differentiated and undifferentiated oligopoly, and also considers the effects that inventories have on the optimal policy. His model has the weakness, however, that price is only defined in relation to some given base period price: the firm decides on the magnitude and direction of a *change* in price. We are thus led back to what looks very much like the original kinked demand curve analysis, but by a much more rigorous route.

Clearly there is evidence that literature on the theory of the kinked demand curve will continue to grow. Some of it, as in Holthausen (1979) will represent a new departure (involving in this case a consideration of the effects of risk aversion on oligopolistic pricing), whilst the rest, as in Walters (1980), will involve the re-discovery or re-working of known results. Most probably, as is the case for the majority of the recent works cited, the kinked demand curve will emerge as a side result of a larger theory.

6.2.   *The Current State of the Evidence*

A detailed review of the evidence was given in the preceding chapter. It is clear that empirical tests have not yet been unambiguous. Objective tests of the Stigler type appear to refute the kinked demand curve hypothesis. Subjective evidence, based on surveys, suggests that in at least some oligopolistic markets, the demand curve facing individual firms is kinked at the prevailing price.

An issue that has not yet been resolved is whether list prices provide an appropriate proxy for transaction prices. Means argued that they do for the index he considered, but for some time this claim was disputed. Stigler and Kindahl (1970) have computed their own NBER index and compared this with the BLS index used by Means. Undoubedly some indices are more important for particular purposes than others, and in this sense it is unlikely that an unqualified case can be made for one index over another. Generally the NBER index is subject to smoother changes than the BLS index, and might be regarded as a more satisfactory summary measure. On the other hand, the more jumpy progression of the BLS index is more representative of the movement of any one price series, as an inspection of figures 4-3 and 4-4 of Stigler and Kindahl (1970, 40–1) confirms. Evidence from other countries apart from the U.S.A. is scant, but a major study in the U.K. by Coutts et al. (1978, 138) concluded that 'there was little evidence found to support the view that the wholesale price indices, being composed of listed quotations, do not accurately measure transaction prices'. Undoubtedly the only satisfactory empirical procedure is to use transaction prices, but it is expensive to do so, and in some cases impossible, if firms are sensitive about disclosing information. An advantage of the survey approach is that questions about the kinked demand curve implicitly involve discussion of transactions, rather than list, prices.

A major weakness of the current evidence, both objective and subjective, is that no attempt is made to link measurable price variation to measurable cost variation. A point emphasised by Galbraith and Means was that, given stable demand, if costs did not change, prices should not be expected to change. There is clearly scope for examining the responsiveness of price to cost changes, with a view to determining whether some industries can absorb cost changes without altering the optimal choice of price, as suggested by the kinked demand curve theory.

6.3.   *Testing the Kinked Demand Curve Theory*

It has become clear in the discussions of chapters 4 and 5 that direct, 'objective' tests of the kinked demand curve theory are very difficult to perform. Primeaux and Bomball (1974) have come closest to providing adequate testing of the theory, but even their study has a number of serious deficiencies. Put in fairly general terms, the kinked demand curve theory says that the more peaked is the profit function, the more stable is the equilibrium at the peak, assuming profit maximisation is the motivation of the firm. The existence of a literal kink in the demand curve, rather than a rapid local change in elasticity, is not really essential to this argument, as Stigler (1978) and Loomes (1979) have emphasised. This peakedness of the profit function has various consequences for conventional theories of the firm, one of which has received great emphasis – the variability of equilibrium price.

The simplest version of the argument runs as follows. There are basically three market structures: monopoly, monopolistic competition, and perfect competition. Each of these theories assumes profit maximisation to be the objective of the firm, and monopolistic competition embraces the full range of intermediate cases, including partial monopoly, duopoly and Chamberlinian monopolistic competition, amongst others. Also in this group is the kinked demand curve theory. For analytical convenience, let the kink be regarded as a rapid change in the elasticity of the demand curve, rather than a finite jump. Suppose that costs are subject to variations that may be represented by a continuous one-dimensional random variable ϵ with probability density function $f(\epsilon)$. Let the profit function for the kinked demand curve case be expressed in so-called indirect form, making profit a function of price. Then the profit maximising condition may be expressed

$$R_k'(p) - C_k'(p, \epsilon) = 0$$

where the subscript k denotes the kinked demand curve case, and R and C refer to total revenue and total cost respectively. This may be expressed more simply as

$$F_k(p, \epsilon) = 0$$

which, provided F_k satisfies certain regularity conditions may be solved in terms of p to give

$$p = \phi_k(\epsilon)$$

Price then has a density function given by

$$g(p) = |1/\phi_k'|f(\epsilon)$$

from which the variance of price may be derived

$$\text{var}_k(p) = \sigma_k^2$$

It will be assumed that the variance of price is an appropriate measure of price flexibility, though it undoubtedly is an imperfect one. Then the simplest version of the argument about the effect of the kink on price rigidity asserts that if σ_m^2 and σ_c^2 are the variances of price under monopoly and under competition, then

101

$$\sigma_k^2 < \sigma_c^2, \sigma_m^2$$

That is, price is less flexible with the kink than under conditions of monopoly and perfect competition.

Stated in these terms, there are many missing links in this argument. Most important of all, it is unclear how one proceeds from knowledge of the structure of demands and costs under the kinked demand curve case, to an expression for the variance of price under either monopoly or competition. Presumably the argument underlying the above inequality is of the form: 'If the market were not subject to monopolistic competition of the type that implied a kinked demand curve, but rather to monopoly, or perfect competition, then price would be more variable'. It is an argument that looks deceptively simple. It would require the construction of a model that used the same population of firms, with the same technical relationships, and deriving from it an expression for the variance of price. Scitovsky (1941) has already demonstrated how difficult it is to get a general result for a comparison of price flexibility between firms subject to perfect competition, and a monopoly achieved by bringing these same firms under the ownership of one entrepreneur. In the case presently under consideration, the analytical problem is considerably more complex. For example, suppose one wished to make the comparison between σ_m^2 and σ_k^2. Should it be assumed that product differentiation would disappear in the monopolised case? If so, must one then compare the variance of a single price, with an average of the variances of the prices set by the various firms with kinked demand curves? In making a decision on what might be an appropriate average to adopt, an element of arbitrariness has already been introduced into the comparison. If it is assumed that the monopolist continues to produce the same product varieties as originally existed, the analytical problem of determining the effect this will have on the flexibility of each price is extremely complex, and up to this time has defied solution. Indeed, if the much more simple case examined by Scitovsky is any guide, it is quite probable that little can be said on *a priori* grounds.

Thus even the simplest comparisons of price flexibility prove too tricky. If it is admitted that behaviour under monopoly or atomistic competition may not follow profit maximising assumptions, then the sort of comparisons mentioned above become even more difficult. For example, it may be that a discussion of monopoly in terms of the recently developed theory of Leibenstein (1979) may be more appropriate than the traditional analysis along lines established by Cournot. Leibenstein's theory of inert areas could provide one explanation for prices being as rigid under monopoly as under kinked demand curve oligopoly.

It seems unlikely therefore that, except under very extraordinary conditions, the opportunity for undertaking a valid price flexibility test of the traditional sort will arise. However, the testing of the kinked demand curve theory, as modified by Efroymson, presents far stronger opportunities for empirical testing, involving as it does the examination of price flexibility *for individual firms* over the phases of the business cycle.

Although earlier reactions to survey methods, of the sort pioneered by Hall and Hitch, were largely hostile, the acceptability of such evidence has increased greatly as survey methods have improved. The limited extent of such work so far performed on pricing behaviour has already been highly illuminating, and amongst other things has thrown light on the kinked and doubly kinked demand curve hypotheses. However, the work needs to be considerably extended. The most impressive survey work so far performed on the kinked demand curve and related hypotheses has been that of Nowotny and Walther (1978). However it refers only to Austrian firms, and it cannot safely be concluded that the findings will generalise to any other economies with market sectors. Furthermore, the object of the economist's analysis, unlike that of the physicist, is constantly changing. New products emerge, new forms of firms flourish, and the institutional framework within which economic activity takes place is constantly mutating. Fog (1960) undertook pioneering work on Danish manufacturing, but twenty years later there arises the need for a reappraisal. If the kinked demand curve theory is to merit the continued attention it receives in the training of economists, there is a strong need for a great deal more empirical examination to be applied to it.

6.4. *Final Remarks*

It is probably worth confirming, in these final sentences, the force of Stigler's view that the real point is to suggest, and perform, new tests of the kinked demand curve hypothesis. No amount of analysis of the existing body of ideas can be a substitute for the imaginative formulation of testing procedures. However, it is important to ensure that such testing procedures are built on firm foundations, and that one does not proceed from a basis which is not well secured. In the case of the kinked demand curve theory it seems to the author that the almost ritualistic status it now has in the economic literature has been a positive impediment to the development of appropriate testing procedures. How else can one explain the fact that the earliest articles developing the hypothesis are often quoted alongside the first article refuting the hypothesis, with no attempt to resolve the contradiction? If as a result of this monograph the mechanical developments of the kinked demand curve analysis were to disappear from many text books, and if a more general theory of contingent demand curves, embracing the kinked demand curve as a special case, were to be developed in the literature, the author would feel that his task had been abundantly rewarding. This in turn might make a small contribution to the fostering of a discerning attitude to the testing of empirical hypotheses in the theory of the firm.

Bibliography

Albach, H. (1965) *Käuferverhalten und Preisbildung im unvollkommen Oligopol.* Discussion Paper No.1, Betriebswirtschaftschaftliches Seminar der Universität, Bonn.
— (1979) Market Organization and Pricing Behaviour of Oligopolistic Firms in the Ethical Drugs Industry: An Essay in the Measurement of Effective Competition. *Kyklos 32,* 523-40.
Allen, C. L. (1962) *Elementary Mathematics of Price Theory.* Belmont: Wadsworth.
Andrews, P. W. S. (1949) *Manufacturing Business.* London: Macmillan.
— (1964) *On Competition in Economic Theory.* London: Macmillan.
Andrews, P. W. S. & E. Brunner (1975) *Studies in Pricing.* London: Macmillan.
Bain, J. S. (1949) Price and Production Policies, in Ellis (1949).
— (1952) *Price Theory.* New York: Holt.
— (1960) Price Leaders, Barometers and Kinks. *Journal of Business 33,* 193-203.
Barback, R. H. (1964) *The Pricing of Manufactures.* London: Macmillan.
Baumol, W. J. (1958) On the Theory of Oligopoly. *Economica 25,* 187-98.
Bezanson, A. C., R. D. Gray & M. Hussey (1936) *Wholesale Prices in Philadelphia 1784-1861.* Philadelphia: University Press.
Borchert, M. (1971) Geknickte Oligopolnachfragekurve und Preisstarkheit. *Weltwirtschaftliches Archiv 107,* 153-8.
Boulding, K. E. (1948) *Economic Analysis* (rev. ed.). London: Hamish Hamilton.
Boulding, K. E. & G. J. Stigler, eds (1953) *Readings in Price Theory.* London: George Allen and Unwin.
Braverman, A. (1980) Consumer Search and Alternative Market Equilibria. *Review of Economic Studies 47,* 487-502.
Brockhoff, K. (1968) On Duopoly with a Doubly Kinked Demand Function. *Zeitschrift für die Gesamte Staatswissenschaft 124,* 451-66.
Bronfenbrenner, M. (1940). Applications of the Discontinuous Oligopoly Demand Curve. *Journal of Political Economy 48,* 420-7.
Cecchella, A. (1975) La Curva a Gomito e l'Elasticita della Domando. *Giornale degli Economisti 34,* 95-108.

Chamberlin, E. H. (1933) *The Theory of Monopolistic Competition.*
Cambridge. Mass.: Harvard University Press.

Clark, J. M. (1961) *Competition as a Dynamic Process.*
Washington: Brookings Institution.

Coase, R. H. (1934) The Problem of Duopoly Reconsidered.
Review of Economic Studies 2, 137-43.

Coutts, K., W. Godley & W. Nordhaus (1978) *Industrial Pricing
in the United Kingdom.* Cambridge: University Press.

Cowling, K. & J. Cubbin (1970) *Price Formation in the U.K. Motor
Industry; An Analysis of Oligopolistic Behaviour.* Discussion Paper,
Centre for Industrial and Business Studies, University of Warwick.

— (1972) Hedonic Price Indexes for United Kingdom Cars.
Economic Journal 82, 963-78.

Coyne, J. (1975) Kinked Supply Curves and the Labour Market.
Journal of Economic Studies 2, 139-51.

Cyert, R. M. (1955) Oligopoly Behaviour and the Business Cycle.
Journal of Political Economy 63, 41-51.

Cyert, R. M. & M. H. de Groot (1971) Interfirm Learning and the
Kinked Demand Curve. *Journal of Economic Theory 3,* 272-87.

Efroymson, C. W. (1943) A Note on Kinked Demand Curves.
American Economic Review 33, 98-109.

— (1955) The Kinked Demand Curve Reconsidered.
Quarterly Journal of Economics 69, 119-36.

Ellis, H. S., ed. (1949) *A Survey of Contemporary Economics.*
Philadelphia: The Blakiston Company.

Fellner, W. (1949) *Competition Among the Few: Oligopoly and
Similar Market Structures.* New York: Alfred A. Knopf.

Fog, B. (1960) *Industrial Pricing Policies: An Analysis of Pricing
Behaviour of Danish Manufacturers.* Amsterdam: North Holland.

Galbraith, J. K. (1936) Monopoly Power and Price Rigidities.
Quarterly Journal of Economics 50, 456-75.

Greenhut, M. L. (1967) A Theory of the Micro Equilibrium Path
of the Firm in Economic Space. *South African Journal of
Economics 35,* 230-43.

Grossack, I. M. (1966) Duopoly, Defensive Strategies and the
Kinked Demand Curve. *Southern Economic Journal 32,* 406-16.

Gutenberg, E. (1955) *Grundlagen der Betriebswirtschaftslehre.*
Berlin: Springer-Verlag.

— (1965) Zur Diskussion der Polypolistischen Absatzkurve.
Jahrbücher für Nationalekonomie und Statistik 177, 289-303.

Hall, R. L. & C. J. Hitch (1939) Price Theory and Business Behaviour.
Oxford Economic Papers 2, 12-45. Reprinted in Wilson *et al.* (1951).

Hamburger, W. (1967) Conscious Parallelism and the Kinked
Demand Curve. *American Economic Review* (Papers and
Proceedings) *57,* 266-8.

Hawkins, C. J. (1971) *An Exploration of the Kinked Demand
Curve Hypothesis.* Southampton University Discussion Papers in
Economics and Econometrics, No.7102.

Hawkins, E. R. (1954) Price Policies and Theory.
Journal of Marketing 18, 233-40.

Hayes, H. G. (1928) *Our Economic System*. New York: Holt.

Heidensohn, K. & N. Robinson (1974) *Business Behaviour*. Oxford: Philip Alan.

Hieser, R. (1953) A Kinked Demand Curve for Monopolistic Competition. *Economic Record 29*, 19-34.

Holthausen, D. M. (1979) Kinky Demand, Risk Aversion and Price Leadership. *International Economic Review 20*, 341-8.

Humphrey, D. D. (1937) The Nature and Meaning of Rigid Prices, 1890-1933. *Journal of Political Economy 45*, 651-61.

Kahn, R. F. (1937) The Problem of Duopoly. *Economic Journal 47*, 1-20.

— (1952) Oxford Studies in the Price Mechanism. *Economic Journal 62*, 119-30.

Kaldor, N. (1934) Mrs Robinson's 'Economics of Imperfect Competition'. *Economica 1*, 335-41.

Kilger, W. (1962) Die Quantitative Ableitung dyopolistischer Preis-Absatzfunktionen aus den Heterogenitatsbedingungen atomistischen Märkte, in Koch (1962).

Koch, H., ed. (1962) *Zur Theorie der Unternehmung: Festschrift zum 65. Geburtstag von E. Gutenberg*. Wiesbaden: T. Gabler.

Lancaster, K. J. (1966) A New Approach to Consumer Theory. *Journal of Political Economy 74*, 132-57.

Lange, O. (1944) *Price Flexibility and Employment*. Bloomington, Ill.: Principia Press.

Leibenstein, H. (1979) *Beyond Economic Man: A New Foundation for Microeconomics*. Cambridge, Mass.: Harvard University Press.

Liebhafsky, H. H. (1972) The Geometry of Kinky Oligopoly: Marginal Cost, the Gap and Behaviour: Comment. *Southern Economic Journal 39*, 143-4.

Loomes, G. (1979) *Kinky or Just Bent*. University of Newcastle-upon-Tyne Discussion Paper.

Machlup, F. (1946) Marginal Analysis and Empirical Research. *American Economic Review 36*, 519-54.

— (1952) *The Economics of Sellers' Competition*. Baltimore: Johns Hopkins Press.

Manzetti, F. (1977) Doubly Kinked Demand Curves and Nonrigidity of Oligopoly Price. *Scandinavian Journal of Economics 79*, 361-5.

Markham, J. W. (1952) *Competition in the Rayon Industry*. Cambridge, Mass.: Harvard University Press.

Marshall, A. (1920) *Principles of Economics*, 8th ed. London: Macmillan.

Marshall, L. C., ed. (1921) *Business Administration*. Chicago: University Press.

Mason, E. S. (1938) Price Inflexibility. *Review of Economic Statistics 20*, 53-64.

Means, G. C. (1935) *Industrial Prices and their Relative Inflexibility*. u.s. Senate Document 13, 74th Congress, 1st Session, Washington.

Means, G. C. (1936) Notes on Inflexible Prices. *American Economic Review* (Supplement) *26*, 23-35.

Mikesell, R. F. (1940) Oligopoly and the Short-Run Demand for Labour. *Quarterly Journal of Economics 55*, 161-6.

Mill, J. S. (1848) *Principles of Political Economy* (John Lubbock edition). London: Routledge.

Mills, F. C. (1927) *Behaviour of Prices.* New York: National Bureau of Economic Research.

Moore, H. L. (1922) Elasticity of Demand and Flexibility of Prices. *Journal of the American Statistical Association 18*, 8-12.

Negishi, T. (1979) *Microeconomic Foundations of Keynesian Macroeconomics.* Amsterdam: North-Holland.

Niehans, J. (1958) Kartelle und Preis Flexibilität. *Schweizerische Zeitschrift für Volkswirtschaft und Statistik 94*, 315-28.

Nowotny, E. & H. Walther (1978a) The Kinked Demand Curve – Some Empirical Observations. *Kyklos 31*, 53-67.

— (1978b) *Die Wettbewerbintensität in Österreich: Ergebnisse der Befragungen und Interviews.* Vienna: Orac Verlag.

Ott, A. E. (1962) Preis-Absatzfunktionen beim unvollkommenen Oligopol. *Weltwirtschaftliches Archiv 88*, 287-307.

Pashigian, P. (1967) Comment. *American Economic Review* (Papers and Proceeedings) *57*, 271-2.

Peel, D. A. (1972) The Kinked Demand Curve – The Demand for Labour: Reconsidered. *Recherches Economique de Louvain 38*, 267-74.

Primeaux, W. J. & M. R. Bomball (1974) A Re-examination of the Kinky Oligoopoly Demand Curve. *Journal of Political Economy 82*, 851-62.

Primeaux, W. J. & M. C. Smith (1976) Pricing Patterns and the Kinky Demand Curve. *Journal of Law and Economics 19*, 189-99.

Reid, G. C. (1975) *An Analytical Study of Price Leadership.* ph.d. thesis, University of Edinburgh.

— (1977) Discontinuity Problems in a Generalized Price Leadership Model. *Journal of Economic Studies 4*, 38-44.

Robinson, A. (1939) Review of Oxford Economic Papers 1 and 2. *Economic Journal 49*, 538-43.

Robinson, J. (1933) *The Economics of Imperfect Competition.* London: Macmillan.

Salop, S. C. (1979) Monopolistic Competition with Outside Goods. *Bell Journal of Economics 10*, 141-56.

Scherer, F. M. (1970) *Industrial Pricing.* Chicago: Rand McNally.

Scitovsky, T. (1941) Prices Under Monopoly and Competition. *Journal of Political Economy 49*, 663-85.

— (1978) Asymmetries in Economics. *Scottish Journal of Political Economy 25*, 227-37.

Sengupta, S. S. (1967) *Operations Research in Sellers' Competition: A Stochastic Microtheory.* New York: Wiley.

Shackle, G. L. S. (1955) Business Men on Business Decisions. *Scottish Journal of Political Economy 2*, 32-46.

Shapley, L. & M. Shubik (1969) Price Strategy Oligopoly with Product Variation. *Kyklos 20*, 30-44.

Shepherd, W. G. (1962) On Sales-Maximising and Oligopoly
Behaviour. *Economica 29*, 420-4.

Shubik, M. (1959) *Strategy and Market Structure*. New York: Wiley.

Simon, J. L. (1969) A Further Test of the Kinky Oligopoly Demand
Curve. *American Economic Review 59*, 971-5.

Simons, H. C. (1948) *Economic Policy for a Free Society*.
Chicago: University Press.

Smith, A. (1776) *The Wealth of Nations*, Vol. 1 (Cannan edition,
1904). London: Methuen.

Smith, D. S. & W. C. Neale (1971) The Geometry of Kinky Oligopoly:
Marginal Cost, the Gap and Price Behaviour. *Southern Economic
Journal 37*, 276-82.

— (1972) The Geometry of Kinky Oligopoly: Marginal Cost, the Gap
and Price Behaviour: Reply. *Southern Economic Journal 39*, 144-5.

Smith H. (1935) Discontinuous Demand Curves and Monopolistic
Competition; a Special Case. *Quarterly Journal of Economics 49*,
542-50.

Smith, V. E. (1948) Note on the Kinky Oligopoly Demand Curve.
Southern Economic Journal 15, 205-10.

Spengler, J. J. (1965) Kinked Demand Curves: By Whom Used First?
Southern Economic Journal 32, 81-4.

Stigler, G. J. (1947) The Kinky Oligopoly Demand Curve and Rigid
Prices. *Journal of Political Economy 55*, 432-47. Reprinted in Boulding
et al. (1955) pp.410-39.

Stigler, G. J. (1978) The Literature of Economics: The Case of the
Kinked Oligopoly Demand Curve. *Economic Inquiry 16*, 185-204.

Stigler, G. J. & J. K. Kindahl (1970) *The Behaviour of Industrial Prices*
(N.B.E.R. no.90, General Series). New York: Columbia University
Press.

Stiglitz, J. E. (1979) Equilibrium in Product Markets with Imperfect
Information. *American Economic Review* (Papers and Proceedings)
69, 338-45.

Streeten, P. (1951) Reserve Capacity and the Kinked Demand Curve.
Review of Economic Studies 18, 103-13.

Sweezy, P. M. (1937) Discussion on wage policy and investment in round
table on wages policies. *American Economic Review* (Papers and
Proceedings) *27*, 156-7.

— (1938) *Monopoly and Competition in the English Coal Trade,
1550-1880*. Cambridge, Mass.: Harvard University Press.

— (1939) Demand Under Conditions of Oligopoly. *Journal of Political
Economy 47*, 568-73. Reprinted in Boulding *et al.* (1953) pp.404-9.

Tucker, R. S. (1938) The Reasons for Price Rigidity.
American Economic Review 28, 41-54.

Viner, J. (1921) Price Policies: The Determination of Market Price, in
Marshall (1921) pp.343-7 and reprinted in Viner (1958) pp.3-7.

— (1958) *The Long View and the Short*. Glencoe, Ill.: The Free Press.

Walters, A. A. (1980) A note on Monopoly Equilibrium. *Economic
Journal 90*, 161-2.

Bibliography

Welham, P. J. (1973) *Note on the Kinked Demand Curve.* Department of Economics Working Paper No.3, Heriot-Watt University.

Whitehead, D. H. (1963) Price-Cutting and Wages Policy. *Economic Record 39*, 187-95.

Wied-Nebbeling, S. (1975) *Industrielle Preissetzung.* Tübingen: Mohr (Paul Siebeck).

Willeke, F. W. (1964) Monopolistische und Autonome Preisintervalle. *Jahrbucher fur Nationalokonomie und Statistik 176*, 407-27.

Wilson, T. & P. W. S. Andrews, eds (1951) *Oxford Studies in the Price Mechanism.* Oxford: Clarendon Press.

Zeuthen, F. (1930) *Problems of Monopoly and Economic Warfare.* London: Routledge and Kegan Paul.

Indexes

Author Index

111

Subject Index